Creating Your Career Portfolio

At a Glance Guide

Anna Graf Williams Ph.D.

Karen J. Hall

Prentice Hall
Upper Saddle River, NJ 07458

Library of Congress Cataloging-in-Publication Data
Williams, Anna Graf.
    Creating your career portfolio: at a glance guide/Anna Graf
Williams, Karen J. Hall
    p. cm.
    Includes index
    ISBN 0-13-606815-4
    1. Hospitality industry--Vocational guidance. I. Hall, Karen J.
II. Williams, Anna Graf. Creating your career portfolio.
TX911.3.V62W53   1997   96-41283
647.94'023--dc20   CIP

Production Editor: *Eileen O'Sullivan*
Managing Editor: *Mary Carnis*
Acquisitions Editor: *Neil Marquardt*
Director of Manufacturing and Production: *Bruce Johnson*
Production Manager: *Ed O'Dougherty*
Marketing Manager: *Frank Mortimer, Jr.*
Editorial Assistant: *Rose Mary Florio*
Cover Design: *Miguel Ortiz*
Printer/Binder: *Courier/Stoughton*

 ©1997 by Prentice-Hall, Inc.
A Simon & Schuster Company
Upper Saddle River, New Jersey 07458

> To everyone who is looking to package
> who they **really** are, may you find hope and
> professional success in pursuit of the
> portfolio process

Printed in the United States of America

10   9   8   7   6   5   4   3   2   1

ISBN 0-13-606815-4
ISBN 0-13-754367-0

Prentice-Hall International (UK) Limited, *London*
Prentice-Hall of Australia Pty. Limited, *Sydney*
Prentice-Hall Canada Inc., *Toronto*
Prentice-Hall Hispanoamericana, S.A., *Mexico*
Prentice-Hall of India Private Limited, *New Delhi*
Prentice-Hall of Japan, Inc., *Tokyo*
Simon & Schuster Asia Pte. Ltd., *Singapore*
Editora Prentice-Hall do Brasil, Ltda., *Rio de Janeiro*

Contents

CHAPTER 2—THE DETAILS

Preface

The question you're probably asking right now is—what is a career portfolio? The career portfolio is a tool you use to organize information about yourself, which is then used to help you get a new job, or improve your current position. The portfolio is a zippered, 3-ring binder containing information about your beliefs, experiences, and education. It will contain samples of your work; those developed on the job or completed in a classroom setting. The portfolio may also include lists of skills and competencies you possess.

The portfolio is designed by **you**, to help you present the best of yourself to other people. As a tool in an interview or job review, it can be used to generate conversation about your abilities and interests, demonstrate things you've accomplished, and, more importantly, provide proof of the things you've done. It can distinguish you from the competition and give you an edge. People tend to believe what they can see.

The portfolio can be a powerful tool, but much of its power comes from the **process** behind it. The process of developing your career portfolio doesn't happen overnight. It takes time to accumulate work samples. It takes time to verbalize your beliefs and determine your short and long-term goals. It is a process of seeing what is good in yourself and incorporating this into the portfolio; documenting awards received, memberships obtained, or your involvement in community service. The process of developing the portfolio helps you become better organized, and can give you a greater sense of confidence in yourself, because you have **proof** of your own abilities.

Your career portfolio is a tool for life. As your career grows, your portfolio changes and grows with it. New jobs are added to your résumé, new skills are refined and demonstrated. Your file of work samples will continue to grow and expand, and your goals and management philosophy may shift and evolve to higher levels. Your portfolio is an extension of yourself, and you decide what you will make of it.

The *Creating Your Career Portfolio—At a Glance Guide* gives you guidelines for creating your career portfolio. In this book you'll find:

◆ a list of supplies you need to begin

◆ general guidelines for organizing the portfolio

◆ detailed discussions of information to be included in different sections

◆ pointers on using the portfolio in an interview or job review

◆ a style guide—containing tips for creating better looking text, photographs and videos, as well as other ideas for making the production side of the portfolio process run smoothly

While seeking career advice about what to do, a very wise person once said,"Concentrate on doing your best—the money will follow." Use the portfolio process to show your best. Often, you have distinct and effective skills hidden in employment and non-employment areas. *Creating Your Career Portfolio* is designed to assist you in pulling together your many skills and competencies. It is the combination of these skills that make you uniquely you. We hope that you gain insight into yourself, your career interests, and the marketplace of the late 1990s.

If you have any questions or we can be of assistance, please feel free to contact us via mail or e-mail, or visit our web site at **www.learnovation.com**

Anna Graf Williams, Ph.D.
Karen J. Hall
Learnovation

11438 Cherry Blossom West Dr.
Fisher, IN 46038
email: 103327.2455@compuserve.com

1 THE PORTFOLIO PROCESS

Five or ten years ago, if you were carrying a portfolio to an interview, you were probably an artist. These people carried around samples of their work in big, bulky folios. To the artist, their work and the skill behind it, their style and talents were on display in the contents of their portfolio. To know the contents of their portfolio was to know the artist; the person behind the art.

Today, in the extremely competitive job market of the 90s, with many highly-qualified people competing for the same jobs, employers are looking for new ways to distinguish the excellent people from the average. Having a degree is no longer considered proof of your knowledge, skills, and abilities. Employers are beginning to ask for tangible proof; they want to see physical evidence that shows you possess the abilities you claim. Individuals are also trying to find new ways to distinguish themselves from the rest of the competitors; to find an edge. The career portfolio is designed to do just that; provide proof of your abilities and produce a tool that is distinctly you.

The portfolio you create through this process will show the best of your work, your accomplishments, and your skills to eager employers. As the artist's portfolio showed the person behind the art, so your portfolio will show the person behind the work samples. A portfolio also includes lists of documented skills you possess, awards and achievements you've earned, letters of recommendation you've received, your goals for your future, and your vision and beliefs for the future of your industry.

Once you find "the" job, it doesn't mean that your portfolio should now be thrown into the dark recesses of your closet, only to be resurrected when you want to begin looking for another position. The portfolio is designed to transition with you into your job. As you continue to collect work samples and proof of your experiences on-the-job, you can turn your portfolio into a useful tool during a job evaluation or promotion review. Think of the impact you will have when you enter a review, fully prepared to show proof of your accomplishments over the last period.

In this chapter, we are going to provide you with all the basic information you need to create a career portfolio as we answer these questions:

> **Why do I need a portfolio?**
>
> **What's in a portfolio?**
>
> **What supplies do I need to get started?**
>
> **How will I use this in the job search process?**
>
> **How can I use this in a job review?**

Of course, we suggest you read the rest of the book to absorb all the details, tips, examples and ideas we'll be giving as we expand on these answers.

Organization

This book is divided into five chapters:

Chapter 1: The Portfolio Process—An overview of the whole process of portfolio development

Chapter 2: The Details—A detailed look at each section in the completed portfolio

Chapter 3: The Assembly—Putting it all together; producing the portfolio

Chapter 4: Using It—"Now that I have it, what do I do with it?" Using the portfolio in an interview or job review

Chapter 5: A Matter of Style—Production tips focusing on making your documents, pictures and videos look their best

We've tried to make this *At a Glance Guide* live up to its name. If you like to read books straight through from the beginning, you'll find this book organized in a logical way. If you don't like to read a guide until you need help with a particular step, you're in luck. You don't have to read this book from cover to cover to find helpful information. You'll find an overview to the process in this chapter.

◆ When you are ready to work on a particular portion of the portfolio, look up the specific section in *Chapter 2— The Details,* for more information.

◆ For assistance on developing good looking work samples and documents, refer to *Chapter 5—A Matter of Style.*

◆ When you're ready to put your portfolio together, turn to *Chapter 3—The Assembly.*

◆ Before you go to your interview or job review, reread *Chapter 4—Using It.*

Regardless of how you use this book, you'll find it filled with examples, tips, and ideas that will make the portfolio process truly rewarding.

Why Do I Need A Portfolio?

Proof

In an interview or review setting, a career portfolio provides proof of your skills and abilities. Instead of just talking about what you can do during an interview or job review, show the person your portfolio filled with work samples you've created, lists of skills you possess, letters of recommendation, and your professional goals.

An Edge

Recruiters and managers aren't used to seeing portfolios everyday. While your portfolio contains samples of your work, it also contains important information about you as a person. You can start a lot of interesting conversations that wouldn't be possible without a portfolio in hand. In some cases, having a portfolio can make it easier to stress your strengths in different areas.

It's A Process

The most important thing to remember about portfolio development is that it's a **process**. Of course, the physical portfolio is important, but the time and effort you put into its development is the true investment in your career.

Assembling and organizing samples of your work, developing your management philosophy and career goals, and determining the skills and competencies you want to emphasize, or obtain in a job situation, are key to the production of the portfolio. As you work through these areas, you begin to examine your experiences and education from different viewpoints. You learn to recognize your strengths, and find ways to emphasize these through the portfolio. You also are faced with your weaknesses, and in the process, you find ways to compensate. This process of examining yourself while developing the portfolio can build your confidence, so that there is little, or nothing, that an interviewer or recruiter can ask you that you haven't already thought about.

A Disclaimer

Keep in mind, we don't claim that having a career portfolio is the ultimate answer to the job search blues. Jobs aren't going to fall out of the sky at your feet if you just raise your portfolio above your head. Developing a portfolio will help you get organized and prepared for the job market. During this process you will be examining your wants, your skills, your abilities, your strengths and weaknesses. This should help you feel more confident in your ability to successfully negotiate an interview. Having a neat, well-organized portfolio also projects a professional image back onto you.

What is a Portfolio?

By this time, you may be telling yourself that it sounds like there's a lot of work involved in this portfolio process. "Analyzing yourself, collecting samples, writing goals. . ., can't I just hire someone to do all this work for me?"

The Standard Job Search Tools

First, stop and think about the materials the "average" person creates to get ready for the job search process:

◆ **Résumé**

◆ **List of references**

◆ **Cover letter**

All too often, these are the only materials that people prepare and take with them to an interview. These are also the people who tend to experience major panic attacks when a recruiter asks them to bring a work sample with them to an interview, with only 24 hours' notice. They may spend precious time searching for good examples of work they have completed, when they could be having a good night's sleep.

The Career Portfolio

Now, here's what the possessor of the "power portfolio" brings to the interview:

A zippered, 3-ring binder containing a combination of the following sections:

Statement of Originality and Confidentiality	A brief statement indicating that the portfolio is your work and should not be copied without permission.
Work Philosophy	A brief description of your beliefs about yourself and the industry.

(Continued)

Career Goals	Your professional goals for the next two to five years.
Résumé	A brief summary of your education and experiences.
Skill Areas	Tabbed sections containing information on your skills and experiences related to a specific area such as Hospitality Management, Marketing, Lodging, Culinary, Technology, etc. .

Each Skill Area contains:

Skill Sets
Checklists of critical skills related to this area. As you attain different levels of competency with each skill, an instructor or employer can sign off on your ability to perform the skill.

Work Samples
Physical examples of your work. Projects, reports, menus, etc. Work samples are proof of your competency in this Skill Area.

Letters of Recommendation
Letters of support or reference that verify your abilities in this skill area.

Works in Progress	A brief list of works, activities, projects or efforts which are in the process of being completed.
Certifications, Diplomas, Degrees, or Awards	Copies of certifications, diplomas, and degrees earned. Samples of special awards and recognitions you have received.
Community Service	Work samples, letters of recognition, photos of projects completed, programs and brochures relating to community service projects.
Professional Memberships and Service	Membership cards, citations, and letters related to professional organizations.

(Continued)

Academic Plan of Study	A copy of your plan of study that lists courses you have taken to fulfill your degree.
Faculty and Employer Biographies	Brief descriptions of the people whose signatures appear throughout the portfolio—Who they are, and what they do.
References	A list of people who can verify your character, academic record or employment history

Which person do you think looks more prepared for the interview?

What Supplies Do I Need To Get Started?

Here is a list of supplies that will help you begin the process of collecting and assembling your portfolio. There are two goals here: 1.) to help organize your materials and documents so you can easily customize your portfolio for a given interview or review period; and 2.) to purchase the supplies necessary to make your portfolio look professional.

Purchase These Supplies

◆ **Plastic file tote box** —(1 to 2 boxes) Used to store work samples, materials, etc. . Should be able to hold hanging file folders.

◆ **Hanging file folders**—20 to 30 folders.

◆ **Zippered, 3- ring notebook**—Cloth, leather, or vinyl with 1 1/2" to 2" rings. Cloth is the cheapest, ranging from $7-$20. Vinyl costs $20-$30, and is available at local office supply stores. Leather binders often run from $60 or more.

◆ **Sheet protectors**—Clear, plastic 3-hole punched pockets that hold documents and work samples. They protect your portfolio and give it a professional look. Avoid the non-glare variety; they are harder to read.

- ◆ **Connected sheet protectors**—3-5 sets of sheet protectors, bound together in sets of 5 or 10 sheets. These are great for keeping projects and work samples neatly together in your file box. This makes it easier to swap work samples in and out of the portfolio.

- ◆ **Extra-wide 3-ring tabs with labels**—Page protectors are wider than ordinary 3-ring tabs. You need to find extra-wide tabs made for use with page protectors.

- ◆ **Clear printer labels, 1" x 4"**—Used for printing the Faculty and Employer Biographies and creating labels for tabs.

- ◆ **Paper**—Use a high quality paper. See *Chapter 5—A Matter of Style*, for suggestions on paper choices.

- ◆ **Business cards**—Blank sheets of cards are used to create exhibit cards for work samples. You don't have to use plain white cards—select something that shows your style.

- ◆ **Photo sheet holders**—Plastic sheets that can hold vertical and/or horizontal pictures.

- ◆ **Name plate or vinyl card holder**—Used on the cover of the portfolio to identify it as your property.

- ◆ **Zippered pouch**—(optional) Holds videos.

- ◆ **Diskette holders**—(optional) Holds project diskettes.

Have Access To This Equipment

You should plan on using the following equipment when you create documents and work samples. The use of these tools will enhance the quality of your presentation:

- ◆ **Computer**—You should have access to current versions of word processor, graphic presentation, and spreadsheet packages.

- ◆ **Printer**— laser or high-quality ink jet

- ◆ **Color flatbed scanner**

- ◆ **Color copier**—Used to reproduce work samples, certificates, awards, etc.

- **Camera**—Used for photographing work samples and other activities.
- **Video camera** —Videotape yourself in action when necessary.

Things You Don't Need
- **Ink pens**—Do everything on a computer.
- **3-hole paper punch**—Use page protectors instead of punching holes. Your work will look more professional.
- **Paper clips, staples and tape**—If you want to connect several pages or display a work sample, use a set of connected page holders.

How Will I Use This in the Job Search Process?

Here are the basic steps you will take to create your career portfolio and to make the "Sale of a Lifetime."

Steps for the Job Search

1. Save work samples from school and places of employment, secure letters of recommendations, and document community service. **

2. Write your work philosophy and your career goals. **

3. Write your résumé. **

4. Secure feedback on your résumé from friends, faculty, and career placement—revise if necessary.

5. Research the companies you will be interviewing with and scan for employment opportunities.

6. Write cover letters.

7. Send out cover letters /résumé packets both by mail and electronically.

These items should be periodically updated or customized to the needs of the interview.

8. Organize work samples, letters of recommendations/accommodation, and community service documentation.**

9. Do the follow-up calls a week after sending packets with the goal of obtaining a phone interview and/or in person interview.

10. Send a thank you note and follow-up on any questions you have for the interviewers.

11. Assemble your portfolio.**

12. Go on in-person interviews.

    ♦ Take your portfolio.
    ♦ Take extra copies of your résumé and list of references.
    ♦ Take a list of questions about the company.

13. Send thank-you letters for being interviewed.

14. Participate in a second round of interviews.

    ♦ Take your portfolio.
    ♦ Take extra copies of résumé and list of references.
    ♦ Take a list of questions about the company.

15. Send second thank-you letters for being interviewed.

16. Receive the offer in the mail or in person.

17. Value the offers and options.

18. Take the position and launch your career.

**These items should be periodically updated or customized to the needs of the interview.

How Will I Use This in a Job Review?

If you already have a job and you want to shine in a performance review, or want to have an edge in the promotion process, use these steps to advance your career.

Steps for Growing Your Career

1. Save work samples created since your last performance appraisal, secure letters/memos of accommodation, and document community service. **

2. If necessary, update your work philosophy and your career goals; both outside and within the company. **

3. Update your résumé. **

4. Organize work samples, letters of recommendations/accommodation, and community service documentation.**

5. Assemble your portfolio one week prior to your review.**

6. Check with supervisor, offer portfolio 2 to 3 days prior to meeting for performance appraisal review.

7. Go to performance appraisal review and take your portfolio.

8. Continue to save work samples.

**These items should be periodically updated since your last performance appraisal (Note that if the supervisor is new, include highlights since your employment with this company.)

I Need a Portfolio Now!!!

"Oh, it won't take that long to put it together."

"I have one that I used last time."

"My interview is tomorrow and I have to do all this before I can start on my portfolio?"

"Do I update my portfolio, or do I sleep and shower?"

If you've just purchased this book and want to put together a portfolio for an interview tomorrow morning, or if you've had this book for a while and suddenly your interview is upon you, there's still hope. Based on several frantic experiences of our own, rest assured you can put together a basic career portfolio in three hours if you have a computer, printer, and your best friend's help.

Run to the Office Supply Store and Buy:

◆ Zippered, 3-ring binder

◆ Clear page protectors (a box or two of 50)

◆ Extra-wide page tabs

◆ Plastic stick-on business card holder for front of portfolio

◆ High quality paper

◆ Extra ink cartridge (if you're using an inkjet printer)

Grab your Best Friend and:

◆ Your box of work samples or file of projects

◆ A computer and printer

◆ Your most recent résumé

We can't stress enough the importance of having a friend help you with the assembly process. Friends can help you make wise choices for work samples, determine your management philosophy and goals, stuff paper into page protectors, make up tabs and exhibit cards, and help you through this somewhat frantic time. A good friend serves as a sounding board, and tends to ask questions of you that you wouldn't think of yourself.

Include These Sections In Your Portfolio:

◆ Work Philosophy

◆ Career Goals

◆ Résumé

◆ Skill Areas—Determine different areas. Place work samples in appropriate areas.

◆ Letters of recommendation (if available)

◆ List of professional membership and awards

- ◆ Community Service—Any work samples and letters available.
- ◆ References

Don't Forget To:
- ◆ Create tabs for each section
- ◆ Make up exhibit cards for your work samples on plain paper.

See Chapter 2—The Details for specific guidelines for each of these sections.

Sounds Great—But It Won't Work for Me

"Sounds great but it won't work for me." If there is something in your gut that makes you uneasy with the prospect of developing a portfolio, there are two possible explanations. First, you may be a master procrastinator and this is your normal response to work efforts. The second, and more likely possibility, is that you can't see yourself with enough work samples to make the portfolio process work.

Throughout the development of this portfolio process, several participants kept telling us— "this sounds great but . . " Your persevering authors kept trying to figure out the reasons for their resistance to the process. Was it too much work? Were they unsure about how to actually use it in an interview? Finally, after observing one person's struggle during a full-time job search , we discovered the problem. Our friend George was applying for jobs to which he was not well matched. When we probed further, he wanted a job, and was willing to do most any type of work. George had a solid, formal education and lots of community service background, but he kept blocking when we offered to help him put together the portfolio. This went on for months. Then all of a sudden, one employer said, "Could you do a presentation for us and bring us some of your work to the interview tomorrow?" We followed the guidelines in the *I Need a Portfolio Now!* section, and helped him create a portfolio for the next day. He admitted that, "It was the only way to organize my work."

George found that the process wasn't so bad, and worked well in the interview. When we quizzed him about what it was that kept him from doing it earlier, he said, "Most of the 200 résumés I sent out were for jobs where I didn't have an exact match to the company." He felt that the portfolio worked best when you could match your work samples to the skills needed by the company.

The story continues. In subsequent interviews he used his portfolio each time. George said, "Most people conducting the interview don't know how to get information out of you. This portfolio stuff works because you can prompt the interviewer to ask better questions." In several interviews, George found that the interviewer wasn't very interested in the portfolio at the beginning of the interview, but when he used it to answer a question about his experience, it peaked the interviewer's curiosity enough to look through the whole portfolio. Every time he was asked how well the portfolio worked, he would say, "It blew them away—they were impressed."

We're happy to say George found a job where his talents and experiences could be well used. "I might have still gotten this job without it," he said, "but the portfolio made the interview go more smoothly. The interviewers were impressed by the portfolio, and it made me a more visible candidate."

The moral of the story is . . . if you are feeling overwhelmed and uneasy about the portfolio—be sure you are seeking out positions that are really you.

Sounds Great—But I Don't Need It, I Have Lots of Job Offers

"The job market is real good right now and I have lots of offers." If this sounds like you—Congratulations! It would be easy to take the path of least resistance here. Consider however, that using the portfolio may help to "*up the offer.*"

Remember that getting the job is the first hurdle, keeping it is the next, followed by the goal of getting promoted and rewarded for the job.

When you have a portfolio, you have your professional goals spelled out. You can use this section, along with your work samples, to get more money or better benefits. Kate developed her portfolio after receiving three offers to help justify her negotiations for benefits and perks. The money being offered may be preset, but the benefits package can often be expanded for secondary benefits. Secondary benefits are the non-insurance and retirement benefits. She used her portfolio to demonstrate her abilities and her need for professional development. Each of these companies agreed to pay for her professional memberships and one three-day professional meeting. This would save her an average of $1,200 out-of-pocket expenses per year. She was also able to convince her eventual employer to purchase an additional copy of the software they used in the office, for home use. This made her job easier by having the same software at home to do her work.

There is something about the portfolio process which causes you to reflect on who you are, what you want to do, and to search out what you are good at doing. Let's focus on getting you rewarded for your work. Using the portfolio process for *upping the offer* in the interview sets you up to use it on the job during your performance appraisals or year-end reviews.

Read On

You now have the basic ideas necessary to create your portfolio. For a more detailed explanation of each portfolio section, read on.

2 THE DETAILS

This chapter provides the "details" on each tabbed section of the portfolio. For each section, you'll read an overview, and then you'll find the following information in most sections:

Creating the Portfolio—Ideas and suggestions for developing the portfolio

Related Areas—Other sections of the portfolio that are affected by this area

Interview/Review Uses—Suggestions for using this section of portfolio during an interview or review

We've organized these sections as you would position them in the completed portfolio. This doesn't mean you will be developing your materials in this order; quite the contrary, you have to make the most of the opportuities at hand. You'll probably be saving projects and papers or securing signatures for skill areas long before you focus your résumé. Refer to *Chapter 3—Assembly* for tips on organizing and creating the actual portfolio.

The portfolio provides:

Insight into you as a person

◆ Statement of Originality & Confidentiality
◆ Work Philosophy
◆ Goals

A summary of your portfolio

◆ Résumé

Proof of your abilities

- Skill Areas containing:
- Skill Sets
- Work Samples
- Letters of Recommendation
- Certifications, Awards, Degrees, and Diplomas
- Works in Progress

Your commitment to your own personal and professional growth

- Community Service
- Professional Memberships

Reference materials

- Academic Plan of Study
- Faculty and Employer Bios
- References

Statement of Originality and Confidentiality

This one-page sheet should be placed at the beginning of your portfolio. It states that the portfolio is your work, and indicates if certain portions of the portfolio should not be copied.

Statement of Originality and Confidentiality

This portfolio is the work of James Cook. Please do not copy without permission. Some of the exhibits, work samples, and/or service samples are the proprietary property of the organization whose name appears on the document. Each has granted permission for this product to be used as a demonstration of my work.

Work Philosophy

A work philosophy is a statement of your beliefs about yourself, people, and your outlook on life in your industry. Your work philosophy is often used by an interviewer to see if you match a company's corporate culture. After reading this statement, a potential employer should know whether you will fit the "style" of the organization.

Make sure you have a friend to assist you when you're ready to develop your work philosophy. Your friend can help you to take your beliefs and the ideas that you have internalized, and verbalize it to paper. Many people know in their hearts what they believe, but they've never put it into words. Your work philosophy might also be called a management philosophy.

Creating the Portfolio

- **Think about it** —Don't expect to "whip out" a work philosophy or personal mission statement in 10 or 20 minutes. It usually takes a few days' worth of thought and reflection before the "final draft" is ready.

- **Place your most important belief first** —Your work philosophy should be unique to you, communicate who you are and what makes you different from others who may want the same position.

- **Length** —Your work philosophy should be one to four sentences in length, and address your beliefs and your outlook on people.

- **Use bullets** —Consider using bullet points for added clarity.

- **Have a friend review it for clarity** —After you have it on paper, ask a few friends to read it for clarity—not approval. Remember that your work philosophy is never right or wrong; it represents your key beliefs and values.

Sample

Here's the work philosophy of one graduating student:

Work Philosophy

- The customer always comes first
- Financial and operational controls must be clear to all members of the company
- Technology will be critical in reaching the guests and communicating within the company
- I want to be part of a winning team

Interview/Review Uses

- Your philosophy should lead the reader to begin asking questions about your professional goals.

Goals

Your goals set a direction for your career and are general in nature. The goals in your portfolio should focus on the professional achievements, skills, and knowledge you want to acquire over the next several years. Companies use these goals to anticipate your developmental needs and interests. They also show management and recruiters that you do indeed have a plan for your future.

Here again, a friend can help you develop your goals. They can ask questions that make you think about your goals, and help make sure your goals make sense.

Creating the Portfolio

- **Plan your goals for two to five years from now —** When writing goals, think ahead several years beyond today. What do you want to be doing in two years? What do you want to have accomplished four years from today? Goals written for one year or less are often too narrow in focus, and usually concentrate on learning a new position rather than planning for the future. You should also make sure your goals are not so specific as to imply only a narrow interest in the industry or in a specific job. If you are starting in an entry level position, think about the job you want to be doing in two to three years. Goals can help share your vision for where you fit in the organization in the future.

◆ **Make your goals measurable** —Your goals should be specific enough that you will *know* when you've achieved them.

Too broad:
"To hold a position where I can work with people"

Good:
"To develop active relationships with customers and clients"

◆ **Goals are different from Career Objectives** —Career objectives are broad and set a direction for your career. Goals are more specific; they include shorter range objectives that are measurable.

◆ **Write three to five goals** —If you only write one or two goals, you may appear unfocused and give the impression that you're not really interested in advancing your career.

◆ **Don't make your goals too personal** —Goals such as losing weight, attending a wild orgy, or winning a marathon can alienate your interviewer; it may give the person more information than he/she may want to know about sensitive topics. Keep your goals professional and related to your career.

Sample:

Here is a sample of goals which are appropriate for individuals just starting their careers:

Two-Year Goals

◆ To hold a leadership role in my department

◆ To hold at least one active professional membership

◆ To further develop my computer application skills as they apply to controlling costs

◆ To earn the customer service award

- To apply my creativity to develop new menus

Related Areas

- **Work Samples**—You should include work samples that suggest you have already started on your quest to achieve your goals. The best use of your goals is to list your professional and personal development intentions.

Interview/Review Uses

- Use your goals to transition the reader from your career objective on your résumé to your portfolio.

Résumés

Everyone knows about résumés. They are the most common vehicle used in the job-hunting process, and are used to convey information about your experiences and qualifications. A résumé usually contains a survey of your education, work experiences, and qualifications for a position. When used in conjunction with your portfolio, the résumé serves as a springboard for introducing your portfolio into the conversation. It is also provides a summary of the contents of the portfolio.

This section gives general suggestions for creating your résumé. For more details, check out your local bookstore. You'll find dozens of books specifically designed to help you make your résumé look its best.

Most résumés contain the following information:

- Career objective
- Education
- Work experience or skills
- Professional memberships and services held, awards received
- Contact information

- Date of last revision
- Reference list (as a separate document)

Your résumé also needs a line at the bottom of the last page indicating that your portfolio is available for review:

Career portfolio available for review

Types of Résumés

There are several standard ways of organizing a résumé, depending on your experiences, skills and target industry:

- **Chronological Résumés**—Information is organized by date. Information is listed in order of time elapsed, with the most recent experiences first.This is the most common and straight-forward résumé format.

- **Functional Résumés**—This type of résumé is designed to highlight accomplishments and specific skills. It is organized by the different kinds of skills you can perform, such as management skills, marketing, finance, etc. .

- **Performance Résumés**—This résumé type is a combination of the chronological and functional approach. You list employment information in a chronological format, then organize the skills you've developed in each position in order to highlight your accomplishments.

- **Focused Résumés**—This is a tailor-made résumé designed for specific professions such as: teachers, civil servants, computer professionals, lodging professionals, food service operators, etc. . This résumé only lists those jobs you've had which directly relate to the specific area you are targeting. This format is often used by large corporations to track performance and skills within their own organization. If you are looking for promotion within a company, this format may suit your needs. This format is not as popular because it is very specific.

- **Government Résumés**—If you are interviewing for a government position or with a company that contracts with the government, you may be asked to submit a standardized résumé, laid out in a specific format. They are usually narrative in nature, and should use terms from standardized job descriptions and other government documents.

Interview/Review Uses

◆ The résumé is most often used as a starting point for introducing your portfolio during an interview.

◆ The résumé is the first place the recruiter or supervisor will look for your address and contact information. Be sure your address is correct—if necessary, include a local address so the person can follow up on the portfolio.

New Trends in Résumés

Scanned Résumés

These days, you may end up finding a job by placing your résumé in an electronic database, or by creating a home page on the World Wide Web. A growing number of services are now available which will scan in your résumé and place it on the Internet or other database services.

Some services will scan in your résumé and ask you to complete a brief application, including items such as salary preferences, employers, willingness to travel, distance willing to travel, etc. . The service gives employers access to "at a glance" peeks at your résumé. For a fee, they will give an employer a copy of the entire résumé via fax. After that, it's up to the employer to contact you.

Some of these services will provide you with feedback on who requested your résumé and salary ranges other professionals with similar skills are earning in the industry. They will also identify trends in professional fields, such as a need for increased computer skills for Restaurant Management.

Professional databases are available to not only college graduates, but also to professionals trying to determine the marketability of their skills. You can find these databases by browsing on the Internet using key terms such as **career**

placement, job search, and **employment.** Within the databases, you can search for openings by experience, salary ranges, key interest areas, etc.. For using these services you will sometimes pay a flat fee of $25 to $75. In other cases, your résumé is scanned in for free and the employer pays for access.

You'll need to make some adjustments to the look of your résumé before it is scanned. Here are some things to keep in mind:

◆ Use black ink on white paper

◆ Don't use italic, bold, or underline

◆ Use 12 to 14 pitch font size for body text and 16 to 18 pitch fonts for headings

◆ Place your name on each page in the header or footer

◆ Use one-inch margins all the way around the document (During the scanning process, margins are sometimes trimmed and information could be lost with a smaller margin.)

◆ Identify dates and times you are available at different contact addresses. Include E-mail addresses where possible.

◆ Artificial intelligence may be used to screen your résumé. Using the vocabulary and terminology of your industry is critical. Using terms like "dollar volume," "number of people supervised," "franchise vs. corporate owned," etc., might allow your résumé to be selected over another.

Web Page Résumés

More people are now putting résumés on-line with their own web pages. The really savvy people are creating more than just résumés, they're creating on-line portfolios. It's especially critical that your résumé be well developed so you can focus the person searching your page. Links and key terms are critical.

In many cases, you need a résumé that can be sent as a text file via e-mail. There are still a number of people using "snail mail," (U.S. Postal Service) so if you fax or e-mail your résumé, always follow it with a hard copy through the mail.

Skill Sets

What Are Skill Sets?

By now the pieces of the career portfolio puzzle should be starting to show the big picture. As a matter of fact, skill sets are much like a puzzle. They consist of a frame, single pieces, and several pieces that fit perfectly together. Think of a skill set as the big picture frame, a single piece as a skill, and several pieces together as a competency. Skill sets will serve as the foundation of your portfolio. You will use the skill sets to choose your strongest and appropriate work samples.

Skills are things you can do. Chew gum, walk, tie your shoes, gas your car, and operate a computer. Competencies are several skills performed together, like parallel parking a car—you need to have the skill to operate the car forward, the skill to operate the car in reverse, the ability to steer and judge spatial relationships to the curb. Skills and competencies, in a related area, are placed together on a list to create a skill set. A skill set is used to show employers what you can do. Skill sets are a master list.

What Are Skill Sets Going To Do For Me?

Ask not what your skill sets will do for you but what they will do for your employer. Remember that skill sets are not only a list of your abilities, but also show the *level* of your abilities. Skills and competencies should be graded by ability. Many skill sets will work with each skill or competency using three levels of ability:

Awareness—Has awareness of the knowledge/skill, and has completed the task at least once.

Practicing—Is able to follow a guide to complete a task.

Mastery—Is able to consistently perform the task without effort.

How Do I Get Skill Sets?

There are basically four different sources of skill sets:

◆ Industry professional association skill sets

◆ Certification skill sets (those packed with a certification program)

◆ Personally created skill sets

◆ A combination of all of the above

The key to skill sets is that you have a signature from a professional in industry or education who testifies to your abilities. As you progress in the level of abilities of a particular skill, an instructor or employer places his/her signature in the appropriate box, indicating your skill level and the date. It is important that you take responsibility for getting your skills measured and signed-off on. This is especially critical if you do not have a lot of work samples to support those skills. It is always more difficult to get a signature after the employment or class is over, since the person being asked to sign-off may not have as clear a memory of the work. Be sure to request biographical information at the time of signature (See the Section on Faculty and Employer Biographies).

How Do I Create Skill Sets?

Getting started is easy. . . but takes some time.

◆ **Use job descriptions to identify skills you want to have**—Not all job descriptions are well written, however there are usually key abilities identified in the text. Shop through the job requirements and evaluate your skills against those, looking for terminology. In fact, a really great way to self-evaluate your own skills is to write the job description for your ideal position and then check if you meet the qualifications. The Career Development office at your local community college, university, or professional association may be of some assistance if you are not quite sure where to look for job descriptions.

◆ **Use the "Want Ads" or job postings to identify and check skills**—Wants ads in the newspaper or on the Internet tend to be brief because they are paid for by the word. However, this does not devalue the interesting information about the jobs that are available. Look at the skills written and implied. Often times it is right in front of you. Check the Sunday papers and the Tuesday edition of *The Wall Street Journal* for job advertisements.

Now expand and refine this list of skills . . .

◆ **List the things you have done on the job**—If the majority of your work experience is as an hourly employee (line-level) then you need to reflect on a "day in your life." If the majority of your work experience is as a supervisor then you need to reflect on a "week in your life." If the majority of your work experience is as a manager then you need to reflect on a "month in your life." What is this reflect stuff? List all the things you do in the course of a day . . . week . . . month. This usually covers your routine skills. Break your time down so that you can clearly think through the entire period of time. Your list should be of tasks and activities that you do. Try to be very specific, rather than just saying, "as a supervisor I work with people to prepare food for the restaurant," consider also your responsibility for sanitation, coaching employees, and assuring the standards of the operation. Can you do each person's job if asked? Many times we underestimate all the skills and tasks that you do in a day.

◆ **List unique skills**—things special to the position, those things you get asked to do because you are better at it than others. Focus on your creative skills, your problem solving skills, and your ability to do several things at once.

◆ **List your generalizable skills**—those which can be used in many different positions. Consider your technology skills, more and more positions are specifically asking you to prove your computer skills and specific software expertie. Some companies are even giving skill tests to verify your abilities.

◆ **Cluster skills together**—Here is a list of baseline skills and competencies established by the Department of Labor known as SCANS. Use this skill list to review and organize your own skills. Use your review to group like things together:

SCANS

The Foundation—Competency Requirements:

Basic Skills	Thinking Skills	Personal Qualities
reading	thinking creatively	individual
writing	making decisions	responsibility
arithmetic	solving problems	self-esteem
mathematics	seeing things in the	sociability
speaking	mind's eye	self-management
listening	knowing how to learn	integrity
	reasoning	

Competencies—Effective Workers can Productively Use:

Resources	Interpersonal Skills	Information
allocating:	working on teams	acquiring and
time	teaching others	evaluating data
money	serving customers	organizing and
materials	leading	maintaining files
space	negotiating	interpreting and
staff	working well with	communicating
	people from culturally	using computers to
	diverse backgrounds	process information

Systems	Technology
understanding social,	selecting equipment
organizational, and	and tools
technological system	applying technology to
monitoring and	specific tasks
correcting performance	maintaining and
designing or improving	troubleshooting
systems	technologies

from SCANS—Secretaries Commission on Achieving Necessary Skills. 1991 U.S. Department of Labor

How Many Skill Sets Do I Need?

Enough to get the position you want. You may be asking if any skills are assumed, but usually it is better to have proof. Remember that you need to put together true skill sets that describe your abilities and the levels of each of those abilities. Your résumé will show the working time frame and your work samples will describe the specifics.

Use the skills sets that apply to you—Not everything you have done in class or on the job may specifically translate into a skill; you could be doing part of a task, or a series of tasks. Work yourself up to the Awareness level of ability for each skill set you use. Before attending a class or starting a work project, discuss the skills and competencies you want to develop with your instructor or supervisor. He or she can help you map out the skills and levels you want to attain. Be sure to ask for the bio of the professional you are working with so you can include it on the Faculty/Employer Bio Sheet. Your credibility will be established by the professional signing off for you. Be sure to establish their credibility first.

Do Skill Sets Really Have Value?

Yes, skill sets have value because they serve as proof of your skills. Just getting signatures on the attached sheets won't fulfill the process of "proving your skills." Consider these skill sets and categories as a starting point. If you would like any assistance in customizing and developing additional skill sets, feel free to contact the authors.

◆ **Skill sets must be organized and orderly**—If the skills and competencies for an area build on each other, organize them using a hierarchical or chronological order.

◆ **Formatting a skill set area**—Remember that you want measurable, yet broad categories within skill areas. For instance, the ability to check in and check out a guest at the front desk of a hotel might have 28 possible steps in the correct, standardized procedure. You would not list all 28 steps, rather you would list the competency as:

"The ability to check in and check out a guest at the front desk using the manual system." In this statement, you are combining 28 different skills into one competency.

Remember that skill sets are the basics for choosing and organizing your work samples.

A typical format for skill sets would be to have them in clean, clear, concise statements followed by sign-off boxes for signatures. Here is a sample of the computer technology skills for an entry level position in most industries:

Computers & Related Technologies

Awareness	Practicing	Mastery
Has awareness of the knowledge/skill, and/or has completed the task at least once.	Is able to follow a guide to complete the task.	Is able to consistently perform the task without effort.

Is able to load software.

print name	print name	print name
signature	signature	signature
date	date	date

Is able to do file management in a Windows environment.

print name	print name	print name
signature	signature	signature
date	date	date

Is able to create and send e-mail.

print name	print name	print name
signature	signature	signature
date	date	date

Is able to complete work using a word processing package.

print name	print name	print name
signature	signature	signature
date	date	date

Is able to complete work using electronic spreadsheets.

print name	print name	print name
signature	signature	signature
date	date	date

Is able to complete work using presentation software.

print name	print name	print name
signature	signature	signature
date	date	date

Is able to access the Internet and the World Wide Web using a browser and/or specific address.

print name	print name	print name
signature	signature	signature
date	date	date

Is able to send files via modem.

print name	print name	print name
signature	signature	signature
date	date	date

Is able to learn new software and existing upgrades.

print name	print name	print name
signature	signature	signature
date	date	date

(Sample Skill Set)

What Do Skill Sets Do For Me That Work Samples Do Not?

◆ Skill sets are clean, clear, concise statements of your abilities. They are more complete and detailed than your résumé and they give an efficient snapshot of your abilities by reading through a list. Skill sets are a way to document your abilities when you lack specific work samples.

◆ Overall, skill sets are a great way for an employer to see your abilities all laid out. But more importantly, it is a great way to keep track of your own skill progress on a personal level . Once you set up your first skill sets you can better set goals for the skills you want to get and the combination of skill sets you may need to move a job into a career.

Skill Sets are the result of someone, somewhere, trying to prove something and then measure it. They are statements of abilities and knowledge in specific areas, and are used to benchmark or track your abilities and knowledge.

Interview/Review Use, Or . . . How Will I Use My Skill Sets Once I Get Them?

◆ **Use skills to create your professional goals**—If you are using pre-existing skill sets, you can shop through skill sets to create your two- to five-year professional goals.

◆ **Use SCANS skills to help create your own skill sets**

◆ **Customize your skill sets based on your coursework**— While you are in school, take time at the beginning of each term to review the skills and competencies you expect to secure, refine, or learn about in each course. At the end of the project or class, you will have ability at the Awareness, Practicing, or Mastery levels. Imagine going into a class knowing what you want to get out of it, and working with the instructor to create your own learning plan. You want to be in a position to be proactive rather than reactive to your education. This keeps you from being a "passive user" of the educational system. If you don't know where to shop for skills, you may want to start with the SCANS list of foundation skills and work competencies. (Remember to keep good work samples for possible use later.)

◆ **Professionals on the job**—At the beginning of a job, or review period, you should clearly decide what skills you *have, need,* or *want* to prove, and which ones you want to develop during the next year. You need to give yourself enough structure so that you can grow within the company, and as a professional in your field. Consider incorporating your skill needs into your performance goals for the year. This is a good way to strategically organize yourself, especially if you make sure your goals and the company goals interface, or map back to each other.

Work Samples

Work samples are one of the most important sections of the portfolio. They make up the major portion of the portfolio and become the most powerful part of your sales pitch.

Work samples are proof of your knowledge and skills. When assembling your portfolio for an interview, you can customize your work samples to match the skills needed for the position. "Wow" a potential employer by showing them examples that clearly demonstrate skills they want to see. Work samples also add to your credibility. Instead of just telling someone what you have done, you can show them.

Sources of Work Samples

Work samples can be found in:

◆ Classroom projects from your major core courses during school.

◆ Materials you have generated while on the job or on an internship or co-op.

◆ Materials completed in community service projects or professional memberships.

Class Assignments

Projects you developed to fulfill course requirements are a great source of work samples. The grade you earned on the project is usually not given in writing, but could be brought up as a point of discussion in the interview. Some examples include:

◆ Real life simulations.

◆ A feasibility study you generated in a marketing class.

◆ The menu you designed for your menu design project or capstone food course.

◆ A business plan you developed.

◆ An advertising campaign you developed as a team effort.

◆ Office or facility designs.

◆ Spreadsheets developed.

Include these items in a class project sample:

◆ The faculty assignment sheet—you may have to re-key it so that it is presentable.

◆ Table of contents for the entire project.

◆ Names of people working on the project.

◆ Assignment summaries.

◆ Why it was generated, the purpose it served.

◆ Executive summaries where possible.

◆ Financial summaries where appropriate.

◆ Pictures.

◆ Multimedia summaries.

◆ What you learned from the project.

◆ Any prerequisites to this assignment.

On-the-Job Samples, Co-Op Projects, or Internship Projects

Work samples may be written projects you generated on the job. Examples include:

- Sections of the employee handbook.
- Departmental operating procedures.
- Programs or systems created.
- Campaigns created or advanced.
- Market research techniques.
- Promotional materials.
- Job projects such as employee newsletters.
- Special events created.
- Multimedia presentations created.

Include:

- A brief list of learning objectives and your supervisor's performance review should also be considered.
- What you gained from this project

Community Service Projects

Service samples may be written projects or pictures of your involvement in community service. Examples include:

- Planned the "Brotherhood Tree of Giving" for the lobby of a hotel.
- Worked on a grant proposal for a day-care facility.
- Planned a menu for a PTA dinner.
- Catered a sit-down dinner for 80.

Include:

- A summary sheet of what you accomplished.
- Results of the project.
- Who helped you.
- A photo if appropriate

Putting it Together

- **Pick the *right* work samples** —Ask yourself the following questions:

- What will this work demonstrate—skills, competencies, or achievement of goals?
- Is this my best work?
- Does it show mastery?
- Am I proud of this sample . . . all or part of it?

◆ **Include a *sample*, not the whole project**—Try to limit yourself to a maximum of 20 pages per project. People don't *want* to read everything.

◆ **Offer the full project** —Add a line on an exhibit card offering the full project:

Full project available upon request

◆ **Identify people who contributed to the project**— When presenting work samples, clearly identify its purpose and everyone who has contributed to the sample.

◆ **When in doubt, leave it out**—Never include a work sample that you are not proud to be associated with, now or in the future. Remember that more is not necessarily better; in fact, it could be the "kiss of death".

◆ **Use a photo summary**—A photo summary of your work may be the best way to relay a work experience. Create photos which show summaries of your work, not just the physical environment. Include pictures of yourself in action with the project.

◆ **Make it look good**—Select the best way to present your work samples; through text, photos, or video. (See *Chapter 5—A Matter of Style* for more information).

◆ **Use grouped sheet protectors for projects**—You can purchase special sets of 5 or 10 interconnected sheet protectors. These keep an entire project sample together, so you can easily switch entire projects in the portfolio.

◆ **Pay attention to confidentiality**—Materials generated on the job are usually the property of the company you were working for at the time you created the material. When you display or show that material, be sure to recognize the owner. If you have signed a confidentiality agreement with a company, you should not include their work in your portfolio.

You may need to leave your portfolio overnight with an interviewer, and prospective employers are known for photocopying some or all of the materials in a portfolio. We suggest you do not include sensitive or proprietary information in your portfolio. Make sure you include the Statement of Originality and Confidentiality at the beginning of your portfolio.

◆ **Have a schedule for updating your collection of work samples**—Develop a routine for collecting materials. If you are in school, you may choose midterm and final exam time to stop and consider which, if any, of your work should be saved for your files. On the job, make a 30- to 60-minute appointment with yourself once every quarter, to take time to reflect on your work over the past months. You should consider completed reports, projects, awards, achievements, or project summaries.

◆ **Keep track of your work samples**—Get a large plastic tote with hanging folders. You should keep original copies of original works, letters of recommendations, letters of accommodation, or certificates of achievement or degrees. You don't need to spend lots of time arranging it; you just need a designated place to keep your materials.

◆ **Include the correct work samples**—The work samples you include in your portfolio will vary, based on the needs of the potential employer. You should have a collection of different work samples stored in your tote or filing cabinet. Each sample should be in its own set of sheet protectors, so you can quickly swap out appropriate work samples as needed.

◆ **Organize work samples into the appropriate skill areas**—Work samples should be clustered by major skill areas. You determine these skill areas either on your own, or by adopting an expert skill set such as those developed by the authors. Each skill area will have its own tabbed section in the portfolio. Each skill area should contain work samples that emphasize that particular area. See the section on Skill Sets in this chapter for more information on organizing the skills areas section of your portfolio.

◆ **Organize work samples within a skill area**—The organization and flow of work samples will vary with each sample. Try to break up text and photos so that the arrangement creates growing interest and peaks curiosity. You may want to organize your work samples in a flow that will show growth or chronological advancement.

◆ **Use exhibit cards**—An exhibit card is a small card containing a brief summary of the work sample. It is placed inside the page protector of the first page of your sample, and helps the reader remember what he/she is looking at and why. We recommend you create exhibit cards for each work sample using a blank sheet of standard size business cards. Format the page on your computer, and include the following information:

♦ Title of the project.
♦ Purpose of the project.
♦ Date of work.
♦ Who worked with you.
♦ What skills demonstrated in keyword format.

Sample:

Marketing Feasibility Study for Franchise Hotel
Fall Term 1996
Group project - Anna Williams, Mark Warner, Karen Hall, & David Morrow
Analysis—Competitive, customer, SWOT

Related Areas

Focus on the skills needed to secure a position and to grow with the organization. If you are unsure what those skills may be, look at the skill sets section in this book, and then include work samples which show competencies simultaneously for as many as possible.

Interview/Review Uses

◆ Work samples are used during an interview to overview your skills during an interview or used as a direct reply to a specific question you've been asked. If an interviewer asked the question: "How much do you know about computers?" you should be able to turn to specific exhibits, work samples or projects you've completed to point to this answer.

◆ Photo collections of work samples can give you the opportunity to talk and explain your planning skills and what you got out of the activity.

Letters of Recommendations

Letters of recommendation from employers, instructors, etc., can provide additional proof of your abilities. Letters provide personal references from people who have seen you perform. You may need to rely more on letters of recommendation when you don't have many work samples, or the type of work you do doesn't facilitate written samples.

Asking for a Letter

You should solicit letters from people who know you and/or your work personally. Instructors, supervisors, owners, presidents, and guests—all can be appropriate references. Whoever you choose should be familiar with your work and be able to judge performance and competency. You should be proud to be associated with these people. If you don't like them, they probably don't like you, and you don't want a letter from them.

You should request your letter of recommendation in writing long before you need it. Your letter needs to help guide the person writing the recommendation focus their letter on key skills and areas of your personality that you want addressed. Ask for the letter while you are close to the event or you still have an opportunity for contact with the person. You should always allow two to three weeks for receiving the letter, as people tend to get busy. It is appropriate to follow up with them a week after your request.

To ask for a recommendation, remember to start with courtesy and manners; say please and thank you frequently, and in a heartfelt way. Remember, these people hold your success in the palm of their hands. Your goal, the purpose of a letter, is to document your performance, have your achievement recognized, and/or to have your abilities summarized. Most people write lousy letters of recommendation. They tend to make the letters too general or generic. You need to help the person you choose to write the letter. When writing your letter, begin by telling the person the purpose of the letter; for your portfolio, for graduate school, for a press release etc. Then, dial in your reference by giving them a list of traits, skills or attributes you want addressed. Here are some examples:

- ◆ Leadership.
- ◆ Ability to work in groups.
- ◆ Ability to self motivate.
- ◆ Ability to meet guest needs.
- ◆ Ability to complete work.
- ◆ Ability to supervisory.
- ◆ Management skills.
- ◆ Creativity.
- ◆ People skills.

(You may want to shop through the standardized skill sets to make specific requests—see the section on Skill Sets.)

The Perfect Letter

The letter should be on official letterhead, should have an ink signature and should not be folded. The recommendation letter you receive should be addressed as "Dear Future Employer." Do not use the generic, open-ended salutations such as "To Whom it May Concern" ... or "Dear Sir or

Madame." It should also include background information on how the reference knows you and how long you have been associated with the organization or project. They should explain how long they have known you and in what capacity.

Don't be afraid to proof their work. If you find a mistake, be humble and ask for a correction.

Letters of recommendation will go in one of three places in the portfolio—work sample documentation, professional service/membership and/or the community service. If the letter is comprehensive, discussing two or more of these sections, include it in the work samples and refer to it in the other area.

Sample Request Letter:

Inside Address

Today's date

Dear Professor Brush:

I was a student of yours last term in your Hospitality Senior Seminar class. I earned an A in your class, so you probably remember me. I will be graduating in May, and I am currently working on assembling my career portfolio. Could you please write a letter of recommendation addressing the following skills:

- ◆ My ability to work in groups.
- ◆ My ability to do presentations.
- ◆ My ability to perform academically.
- ◆ My ability to do electronic spreadsheets.
- ◆ My ability to read an income statement.

It would also be helpful if you could indicate how long you have known me and on what occasions you have worked with me. I would also appreciate it if you could address the letter to "Dear Future Employer."

I would greatly appreciate receiving this letter within the next two weeks. Please call or e-mail me and let me know when it would be convenient for me to pick up the letter. It would be helpful if I could pick up an unfolded letter. Thank you very much for your consideration and all your help. Please feel free to call me if you have any questions.

Sincerely,

David Morrow

David Morrow
1996 W. Peach Blossom Rd.
Warwick, RI 02888
(401)555-6804 - Home phone
e-mail: davidm@machoo.ocean.com

Works In Progress

This is a place to list projects on which you are currently working. You may choose to show parts or modules that are completed enough to demonstrate a skill, competency or achievement. Your list should include:

- Expected completion date.
- Who the work is for.
- What skills or competencies it demonstrates.

Creating the Portfolio

- This section may be very short. It should be clearly labeled "Works in Progress," and can be placed at the beginning of the work samples. You may want to use a bulleted list.

Interview/Review Uses

- Refer to this list of current projects after you have discussed your work samples. It can serve to transition the interviewer or supervisor into more questions.

Certifications, Diplomas, Degrees, or Awards

Remember, you need to prove the things you have done. Including professional certificates related to areas of specialty, such as Novell certification, training certification, continuing education, workshops attended, distinctions, or accommodations are appropriate items to place in your portfolio.

Creating the Portfolio

- **Include a copy of the certificate**—Include a quality photocopy or scanned image of the certificate or diploma as proof and verification. Don't include the original.

- **Include information about the organization presenting the certificate**—The certificate should be dated and have information about the organization. If it does not, add a page with the following items:
  - ◆ Name.
  - ◆ Address and phone of the organization.
  - ◆ Any certification or licensing numbers given.

- **Place the most recent items first**—If you have any citations (not speeding or parking tickets!) for service, include them here in reverse chronological order with most current items coming first. For example, you received the customer service award at work last year, and you received Dean's List this term—place the Dean's List before the customer service award.

- **Be selective**—What goes in here? Everything? No. Show items that will be of interest to your future employer. Do your homework on the interests of the organization you are applying with or currently working for today. Remember that more is not necessarily better.

Interview/Review Uses

- **If you are in industry**—Certificates earned since your last performance appraisal should be included for a year-end review.

Community Service

There ARE Other Ways to Get Experience

You have not really worked in the area the potential employers are for . . . what can you do? Volunteer. People who are not actively in the work force or those people who have been out for a while can use their volunteer projects as a way to demonstrate skills and secure proof, even without having held employment. Go to an organization and offer your services free of charge. Start a project and see it through to the end. Be sure to make it clear that all you want is a letter documenting your time and skills. Then have some fun and test drive, develop or refine your skills.

Women or men who have stayed at home for a couple of years with their children oftentimes feel their skills are rusty. Prior to entering the workforce, allow some time to do some structured volunteering. It could be as a fund raiser or a kitchen supervisor at the YMCA. Seek out a not-for-profit organization and offer your professional skills. It doesn't matter if you are a mechanic, a cook, a graphic artist, or an accountant—offer the skills you feel you need help documenting. One woman was let go because she didn't have the skills that were required in her ever-changing marketing position. So, our heroine, while unemployed, volunteering in the community, secured the skills her employer was looking for and went back to work. She just needed some way of proving her abilities.

In a recent meeting with industry recruiters, several said they look specifically for candidates with community service in their background. They believe individuals who volunteer will be willing to stay a little longer to get the project done. It signals an individual who is interested in giving back and not just taking from the community—even the corporate community. Additionally, community service is another way to create positive public relations. Sometimes, people are hired because of their volunteer connections and earned respect in the local or regional community. Other employers will require employees to do some community service such as big brother, big sister, little league coach, city council members, or serve as the Cancer Society or Heart Association chairperson.

Citizenship, ethics, and one's ability to balance his/her life is becoming more important. Volunteerism shows that you have a strategy for coping with on-the-job stress. Oftentimes recruiters are looking for ways of seeing balance in your life. Community service is one way to demonstrate this.

Creating the Portfolio

◆ It is appropriate to show work developed while serving with or on community organizations or associations. Examples might include photos of events you assisted with, copies of programs you helped develop or deliver, samples of any of the brochures, bylaws or organizational pieces you developed. Remember, the organizations you associate with are a reflection on you—choose causes you are proud to be associated with over time.

◆ As your career progresses, you need to keep your samples up-to-date. Select your most significant contributions as well as those most current from the last 18 months.

Interview/Review Uses

Don't underestimate this section of your portfolio. Here is your opportunity. The person reading your portfolio now has the chance to ask questions about you, your values and beliefs. Be sure you associate with causes you can support. It's important to understand the mission statement of the organization even if it's not printed on the brochure. Be prepared to answer questions about your service and the association or organization.

Professional Memberships and Services

Professional membership and service shows your commitment to the field and demonstrates how you will keep up with the growing and changing knowledge/skills in the field. You should be carrying at least one professional membership at all times.

What professional groups should you belong to? You'll find many professional groups outside your company. Join professional organizations related to your area of business rather than those that are merely social organizations.

Creating the Portfolio

Items to include in this section:

- A list of organizations to which you belong.
- The date you joined.
- Offices, boards or committees on which you've served.
- Appropriate letters of accomplishment.
- Photographs of events or copies of programs where you have provided a presentation or service where appropriate.
- Provide proof of your membership—Use a membership card or a letter from the president of the organization as proof of your membership. If your membership card is your canceled check, use the letter instead.
- Don't use initials to list the organization—be sure to spell everything out. Common mistakes when using initials only could be mistaking the NRA (National Restaurant Association) to be the National Rifle Association.

Sample:

Professional Memberships

- CMA (Club Managers of America) —Member since 1995.
- Marketing Committee Chair—1995-Present.
- Toastmasters, since 1996.

Interview/Review Uses

- Professional memberships allow you to talk about your professional growth and commitment to your industry.

Academic Plan of Study

You may be asking why you need to include an academic plan of study. The answer is really quite logical—you want to promote all the specialized education and/or training you have received. It also helps a potential employer or current employer distinguish between your background and that of other people in the position. Your plan of study defines the courses you took to complete your degree. Remember that each school, college or university has a distinct curriculum—you want your program to be known.

Creating the Portfolio

Look to course catalogs and transcripts for copies of your plan of study. Transcripts give course titles and grades; if your grades are not that great, don't volunteer the transcript. You should, however, indicate that it is available upon request. You can also use the description/presentation in the school bulletin or catalog. You need to show all your courses in your major and related area. Be sure to include the pages with the program, department and degree description as well as the title page and the date. You will find all of this especially helpful if you ever go back to school for an advanced degree.

Before you leave your school, get 10 copies of your transcript and find the copy of the course catalog that governed your degree. You may have to go back to your freshman boxes to find it. Keep the catalog or bulletin in a *safe* place, since these are often expensive to get if you need them in a hurry.

It may be appropriate to include the course descriptions from key classes. You may possibly need to scan the information. Be sure to cite the date of the program and version of the catalog.

Interview/Review Uses

The academic plan of study section is usually only referred to if needed, and may even be overlooked when the person considering you is reviewing your portfolio. You need to have it in your portfolio, just in case.

Faculty and Employer Biographies

Faculty and employer bios are used to give you credibility. The person who signed your skill set sheets or letters of recommendation is giving his/her *word* that you have certain abilities. The faculty/employer bio sheet gives the interviewer background on who these people are, and how they know you.

Creating the Portfolio

A faculty/employer bio sheet should include the following information:

- ◆ Name.
- ◆ Title.
- ◆ Organization.
- ◆ Address.
- ◆ Phone/Fax/E-mail.
- ◆ Areas of Specialty.
- ◆ Date.

◆ The arrangement of bios should be chronological. It is not necessary to repeat a bio for someone, unless they are promoted during the signature periods of your skill sets.

◆ The bio sheet is placed under its own tabbed section in the portfolio, following Skill Areas and Works in Progress. This information can often be standardized and printed on labels.

Interview/Review Uses

◆ Skills sets are in the portfolio so the employer can correlate your skills with the ones needed for the position or job. In the event you are using your portfolio for performance appraisals, it documents the fact that you have specific abilities which are worthy of acknowledgment or reward. You should be able to verbalize your skills and use the written documentation and/or work samples as proof. Be sure to point out faculty or industry bios of the people confirming your ability.

References

You will need three to five references that an employer can check. You should include character, academic, and employment references:

◆ *Character*—Someone you've worked with in the community, such as church, synagogue or mosque, not-for-profit organizations, clubs, and/or associations all can provide good character references.

◆ *Academic*—Professors, teachers, counselors, coaches, and people who know your academic abilities can provide academic references.

◆ *Employment*—Supervisors, managers, human resource people at your current and previous positions can provide employment references.

It is never appropriate to use a peer, subordinate or family member as a reference.

Include the person's name, full title, work address, work phone, fax, e-mail, and, if given permission, the person's home phone. Arrange all references on one page, and signal at the bottom of the reference the skills, competencies, or achievements the person can address.

Sample:

David Morrow - References

Mr. Richard Brush
Lodging Department Chair
Hospitality College
Johnson & Wales University
8 Abbott Park Place
Providence, RI 02903
(401) 598-1000
Fax: (401)598-2000
E-mail: dbrush@laode.com

Home: (401) 555-2911 (hours. 6 p.m. to 9 p.m.)
(Academic Reference, Club Advisor)

Monsignor Robert McCaffrey
Providence Catholic Diocese
8800 Cathedral Square
Providence, RI 02903
Office: (401) 452-5938
Fax: (401) 452- 5937
(Personal Reference, Community Service)

Ms. Fran Bahmer
General Manager
Heartland Catering
RR1, Box 200
Bloomington, IL 61701
Office: (309) 663-1105
Fax: (309) 663-1106
(Employment Reference, Supervisor for three years; summer employment)

October, 1996

If you have more than three references, set up the page in two columns.

You should be certain that each of your references has a copy of your résumé and copies of work samples referred to them. As long as you keep them as a reference, you should forward them with a copy of your résumé each time it is updated. Send each of your references a copy, highlighting the changes.

Now that you have all the details, your next step is to assemble them for presentation. Chapter 3 will take you through assembly.

3 | THE ASSEMBLY

Assembling the Portfolio

OK, you have all your stuff in piles and files—now what? Remember that the first chapter of this book gave you the big picture view on the portfolio. Chapter 2 gave you the gory details of each section in the portfolio (perhaps even more than you *really* wanted to know). This chapter will get you from the pieces to the whole finished product. You won't be ready to assemble until you first gather, sort, secure and update your materials. You will also find special tips for assembling a Performance Portfolio for use in job reviews or promotion interviews.

Step 1 . . . Things to Gather

First things first . . . read this book. It sounds simple, but remember that you can also use this book as you would use a phone book; to look up the things you need to know when you need to know them.

Bring to one central location all your collected materials—consciously collect:

◆ **Office supplies**—(see *Chapter 1—"What Supplies Do I Need to Get Started?"*).

◆ **Your résumé**—(Be sure your name is at the top in bold; use an 18 pitch font—it should stand out on the page and also appear on the second page in the running head.)

◆ **Your work philosophy**—(again, be sure your name is at the top in bold; use an 18 pitch font.)

- **Your professional goals**—(these can be modified to compensate for weak skill areas and are on the same sheet with work philosophy).

- **Your box of work samples** . . . appropriate physical documentation (Are there any old papers or projects that you can find or copy?).

- Certifications.

- Degrees or diplomas.

- Letters.

- Skill sets with signatures.

- Faculty/employer bios.

- Academic plans of study.

- Professional membership cards and service samples.

- Community service accommodations or service samples.

- List of references.

- And don't forget—your *best*

- friend.

A Reminder—begin assembly of the portfolio before you need it! This sounds easy, but it's easy to put it off until another day. If you decide not to choose this option of working in advance on the portfolio, please refer to the Emergency *"I Need the Portfolio Now"* instructions. We promise you'll need them. Even the authors of this book have had to choose between sleep and finishing a portfolio. Be prepared to clean off a big section of the floor for the assembly. If the floor cramps your style, use a table or large desk—just be prepared to find some space on a flat surface.

Step 2 . . . Sorting and Organizing Work Samples

Use the job description, classified ad, and any other knowledge you have of the company or the position to prioritize the skills you will emphasize in your portfolio. Be careful not to choose too general a field such as training or food production as your main headings (tabs). Instead, you should cluster your work samples by small groups. For example, instead of using *Training* as a cluster, you may be better off with a specific training area such as *Front Office* and *Housekeeping*. Once you have clustered your work samples and chosen *only* the "best" from your files, you need to stop and think about all those things you have done where you may be lacking proof. Consider using some of the following items as demonstrations of your skills and competency:

- class projects
- projects or reports demonstrating organization and professionalism
- writing samples
- performance appraisals (include internships/coops)
- computing samples
- certifications
- team efforts
- handouts
- menus
- presentations
- certificates from workshops
- letters itemizing what you have accomplished.

When sorting work and service samples, ask yourself:

- Which skills is the organization looking for with this position?
- What is your best work?
- Which samples show the most skills and competencies?
- Which work samples are the most interesting to you?
- Which work samples use more than text as an exhibit? Do any include pictures?

Remember the Friend

Having a friend there to help you during assembly can be extremely important. Your friend is there to ask the "right" questions and to look at your portfolio from a "different angle." You may find that your friendship will be tested, especially if he or she does his/her job! Their job is of course to ask you the really hard questions that push you to be your best. Your friend is also here to role-play possible answers you may give the interviewer. Don't take things personally; give that friend honest answers even if they are not your best answers. You'll improve through practice.

Once you have organized your work samples you are then ready to develop the support materials that give your portfolio flow.

Step 3 . . . Putting It Together

Now that you have everything gathered, go ahead and put everything that you've prepared into page protectors and into the 3-ring notebook.

- ◆ Begin with your work philosophy and career/ professional goals (you may customize your goals at this point to take the company's direction into consideration).
- ◆ Put your résumé in another page protector behind the work philosophy page.
- ◆ Insert skill set sign-off sheets.
- ◆ Order your work samples and put them into page protectors using the multi-sheet packets for projects of more than five pages. Order the work samples with your best first and then by variety.
- ◆ Insert blank tab sheets to organize logical breaks (do not make the labels for the tabs yet).
- ◆ Insert certifications, diplomas, and degrees.
- ◆ Insert community service samples.

- Insert professional membership certificates and service samples.
- Insert academic plan of study.
- Insert faculty/employer bios.

Step 4 . . . Developing Support Materials

- **Create a statement of originality and confidentiality**—Insert it at the beginning of the portfolio in front of your work philosophy.
- **Develop exhibit cards**—Use business cards to print information about each work and service sample in your portfolio. Slide one card in the front of each work/service sample exhibit. Each card should include:
  - Title.
  - Purpose.
  - Date developed.
  - Names of team who developed it.
  - Demonstrated skills in key word format—use words that are emphasized on your résumé and heading.
- **Create the Works in Progress list using**
- —(This list should be straightforward, and include a timeline, the title, purpose, and key skills.)
- **Create clear, one- or two-word tab labels**—You are the only one who can determine the correct names for the tabs of your portfolio. Intuitively you may already see some logical groupings of your materials and have some titles for them running around in your head. Choose names for the tabs that are clean, descriptive, and informative. Consider the following when determining your tabs. Your tabs should:
  - be a significant area you want to promote about yourself.
  - have adequate work samples or letters of recommendation.

- be significant to the position or employer for whom you are preparing the portfolio.
- be descriptive of who you are.
- round out and transition your viewer to your other skill areas.
- be a logical grouping of materials.

◆ **Create a reference list**—Choose people who can focus on the skills desired by the organization you are interviewing with at this time. Sometimes a company dictates how many references they want—usually three to five references.

Step 5 . . . Check It Out

We hope this was not an emergency assembly of your portfolio, and you have at least 12 hours to proof and let the portfolio *cool*. Here are a few items you should check and recheck:

◆ Read for typos, spelling, grammar and format. If you are not good at this, have your best friend do it.

◆ Talk through the sections of your portfolio thinking about which parts you will elaborate on in an interview.

◆ When in doubt take it out . . . if you are not sure or not pleased with an item—leave it out.

Rules to Follow

◆ Put all papers in the page protectors using both the front and back.

◆ Use colored paper to draw attention to special work or service samples.

◆ Use the same type of paper on your résumé and references (prepare two extra sets of these to hand out during the interview).

◆ Proof everything at least three times.

◆ Never use your originals.

Tips For Creating the Performance Portfolio

When you have a job, your portfolio can help you keep it and get a pay increase or promotion. The overall organization of the portfolio is the same, except that work/service samples are organized in a chronological order, and your professional goals may be organized by your previous year's professional goals and objectives (or the time since your last appraisal.)

◆ **Check your calendar**—Get in the habit of writing down the start dates, benchmarks, and completion dates of projects. Write down any letters of acknowledgment or awards received in your calendar. Months from now you will have a road map ready to read and secure your documentation for the portfolio.

◆ **Stop once a month or so and make two lists of what you have accomplished, planned and unplanned**—If you can't do it once a month, then take 30 minutes once every 90 days and think about your career. Make the appointment with yourself right now; map out the appointments and keep them.

◆ **Set up a file box or file drawer**—At the end of each project make a second copy of it and put it in your file. At the very least, save it on a disk. Remember that setting aside a copy of your work needs to become reflex, it will save you a lot of chasing when you put together your actual portfolio.

◆ **Review the job description for your position**—As far in advance of the review as possible, you should reread the job description of your position. It is good to strategically consider your level of skill in each of the position statements. Use the job description to guide your quest for work samples and skill set documentation. You may even want to consider seeking out some certifications that will document and help you recover from any deficits.

If you don't have a specific job description for your position (and many people don't), the solution is simple. Write one now. Give a copy of your job description to your supervisor and seek his or her input. It is helpful and strategic to establish the criteria of your position before your review.

◆ **Review the performance appraisal standards before the actual review**—It seems simple, but be sure you understand the "rules of the game" at the beginning of the performance period. This may or may not be possible. Some organizations have very general standards or criteria. It is especially true in these cases that you should develop your career portfolio and utilize it for the review. Now that you know the specifics keep it in the back of your mind as you make decisions on your work samples and career activities.

◆ **Concentrate on your skill sets, your work samples and professional activities**—The other parts of the portfolio such as your work philosophy, goals, résumé, awards, and certificates should appear in your portfolio but not be emphasized. The other sections serve as background and quite often are subtle support you provide to refresh the reviewer's knowledge of you.

◆ **Write documentation for other people the way you would like to receive it**—Remember the key elements of good documentation: time frame, skills demonstrated, people on the team, attitude of the individual and what the future projects could be because of this work.

◆ **Put it all together**—Put together this year's work in a chronological order or into the major areas set up in your job descriptions. Then be sure to explain to the person reviewing you that you have put together a self-review. Set your supervisor up to utilize your career portfolio. Never just walk in the door with your portfolio, it could be perceived as a threat.

4 | USING IT

Using the Portfolio During an Interview

Now that you have the portfolio—what do you do with it? It looks good, feels nice, and you survived the assembly process. You may be wondering "How do I use this portfolio?" and "How do I let them (the interviewer or boss) know that I have it?" This chapter talks about using your portfolio:

◆ To set the interviewer up to look at your portfolio.

◆ As an overview of your abilities.

◆ As an answer to a question.

◆ In a performance review.

◆ To obtain a promotion.

◆ When they aren't interested.

◆ When they want to keep it.

How to Set Them Up

Good marketing is required of you and your work. Promote your portfolio ahead of time by placing a note at the bottom of your résumé: *Professional Portfolio Available Upon Request.* You should also refer to the portfolio in your cover letter when communicating with a company. Your portfolio is one of the prominent tools you take to the interview. During the interview, it's important to let the interviewer know within the first 15 minutes that you have your portfolio available. Remember that the portfolio can be used to introduce you, provide an overview of who you are, or as specific documentation for a question you have been asked. Watch the interviewer for signals of which use will be preferred. He or she may want to see your portfolio right away. You should use it to set up the interviewer to ask you the questions you want to answer, and that you can answer best.

Using the Portfolio As an Overview

Now that the stage is set, you need to paint the big picture. Be prepared for a thorough and complete presentation of your portfolio. When using it as an overview, you have the lead in the interview—you can steer the direction of the questions. Take time constraints into consideration. If you have been allotted a 30-minute interview, you should be able to overview your portfolio in 5-8 minutes, unless there are questions being asked.

Using your Portfolio During the Interview

Actually showing the portfolio physically may seem awkward. You may be sitting opposite the person by the time you are ready to show the portfolio. You should get up and stand beside the person to talk briefly through the sections. Make sure your head is not above the interviewer's head. Kneel or bend down to accomplish this. Usually the person viewing it will already be seated. It's difficult to read upside down, so get up and stand next to the person or people interviewing you.(*A gentle reminder*—Women should pay attention to their necklines when leaning over. Both men and women should be sure their deodorant is working!)

- ◆ **Begin by reading the person your work philosophy and professional goals**—(This shows that you have plans and focus—spend a little time here.)

- ◆ **Point out your résumé and remind the person that he or she already has a copy**—(of course you should have a spare résumé tucked in the inside pocket of the portfolio.)

- ◆ **For each additional section, describe briefly what the viewer or reader will find**—Read the exhibit card information on work or service samples. Spend time sharing components of the work or service sample which may not be obvious in your materials. You may have photos with brief captions that need to be expanded upon. You may have sections of projects which need a brief explanation of background. Let the viewer determine how much detail to go into in each section.

◆ **Don't use the portfolio to shut off questions from the recruiter**—Give enough overview to peak the person's curiosity so he or she can ask better questions of you. When you're finished showing the portfolio, leave it in front of the person and return to your chair.

What Can Go Wrong? . . .

Be aware of a person's personal space and hold the appropriate distance from the individual. If you approach and the person backs away, you need to, as a courtesy, back off as well. You may turn the pages, or if the person seems to be "in possession" of the portfolio, you can signal them to turn the page. Some people will not mind you in their personal space, but be sure to manage any and all of your sexual energy if you are getting close to the person.

Usually what follows, after an overview of the portfolio, are better focused questions from the person interviewing you. Remember, the portfolio is the opportunity used to present your skills and competencies.

Answering Questions

The interviewer may have some starched predetermined format which he or she believes will not lend itself to looking at your portfolio. Fear not! If within the first five minutes of the interview the person has not expressed an interest in the portfolio, be prepared to use it as a means for answering a specific question about your résumé. It should be easy to answer these questions because you had to answer the same types of questions during the portfolio development process.

Here are some questions that lead themselves to be answered by a look at your portfolio:

- ◆ **"What are your five-year goals?"** or **"What are your future plans?"** (See the work philosophy and professional goals section.)

- ◆ **"How confident are you on the computer?"** (See the work/service samples with projects that are computer generated, demonstrating the software and skills they want to see such as spread sheets, word processing and data base project or any specialty software.)

- ◆ **"What do you do for recreation or release?"** (Show them your community service section.)

- ◆ **"What was your most difficult class?"** (Show them a work sample from your class)

- ◆ **"Have you ever ...?"** (Fill in the blank and show the person a work or service sample.)

- ◆ **What certifications do you hold?** (See the certifications, diplomas and degrees sections.)

- ◆ **"Have you ever worked as part of a team?"** (Show them the work/service samples sections where you have already noted this on your exhibit card.)

Don't be surprised if the interviewer asks to see the entire portfolio and not just the one section you are showing him or her.

What to Do If They Are Not Interested

You may find that the interviewer has never heard about using a portfolio before. Additionally, they may not want to take the time to review it. Some people fear the unknown.

It is possible that a specific question you are asked may be answered best by showing a work sample or other section of your portfolio. In one case, a young man had the portfolio with him and the group leading the interview did not want to see it. However, part way through the interview he used it to answer one question. This went on to spark an interest in the entire portfolio. By the end of the interview, the team of interviewers were fighting to see it before he left the interview. You must be able to clearly explain what a portfolio is and how it works. Don't be surprised if the interviewer tells you he or she has never seen one before.

Normally, you will be able to find some way to work the portfolio into the interview or review. However, if you do not spark the interviewer's interest, even after a clear offering and explanation of what the portfolio is, you may want to consider that you may not be suited for that type of organization.

What If They Want It or What If They Don't?

What do you do if they want to keep it? It's up to you whether or not you leave your portfolio. If you choose to leave your portfolio, leave it only for a short period of time—24-48 hours. Remember, your portfolio should be a quality copy. At no time should the portfolio have your original copy of anything.

There are advantages and disadvantages to leaving your portfolio with someone. The disadvantage is that they may copy items from it to get ideas to further their business while not specifically following up with getting you hired. On the other hand, if you leave your portfolio, you have created the opportunity to go back and have another contact with the person or company. Before you leave the interview, set a firm time to pick it up. For example, on a Friday noon interview, set the pickup time as Monday noon. Be sure to call and check before picking up the portfolio. You may have peaked their curiosity enough to have them show it to other people. Remember to include the statement of confidentiality in the beginning of your portfolio.

On occasion, human resource people may want to copy your portfolio to include it with your records. You shouldn't hesitate to give permission for your portfolio to be copied, unless you have a proprietary work sample in it. For example, if you have a series of recipes developed for a company that are proprietary, don't give permission for these to be copied. Your exhibit cards should specifically state that this work should not be copied.

Using the Performance Portfolio at the Review

You will use your portfolio to summarize and review your work. The actual techniques of talking the reviewer through the content is the same for the performance review as it is for the interview. Use it to overview your work and performance or use it as a reply to a question. Remember that your career portfolio is a living document and changes as you do.

The first time you present your portfolio, be prepared for the reviewer to show some uncertainty since it may be a very new concept to them. Also be prepared to go through two reviews. One will be at the 5-10 minutes where you mini-present your portfolio prior to the formal review. During this session you explain the organization of your work and how to read your portfolio. Set your supervisor up to utilize your career portfolio. Never just walk in the door with your portfolio.

There are several effective ways to use the portfolio during the actual full review. Consider using it as a way to present your own self-appraisal. Another possible technique is to use it to answer specific questions about your performance patterns. Yet another way, is to use it as a summary tool at the end of the formal process. The key to making the portfolio work is to allow the reviewer enough time with your career portfolio to use it as a guide. Several industries and organizations have found the performance portfolios have been healthy additions to their personnel review process. This is especially true in the hospitality industry and in the computer technology training field, but it is a growing process in most professional fields. Everyone wants proof these days.

Using the Performance Portfolio to Get a Promotion

Now that you know how to use the portfolio during your performance review, let's talk about how to use it during the reviews where you are up for a promotion. Promotions can be new titles, new assignment to different branches of the organization, or simply progression within the company hierarchy. In any of these cases, your portfolio should reflect your work from the period of your last promotion. If that was two years ago, then your work should reflect the last two years. If you have not been promoted as yet, have your portfolio reflect your work from the time you began your employment.

Work samples, should be just that, samples. . . not everything you ever did. Just as in the career portfolio, you need to choose highlights of your best work. Even if something is not able to fit on an 8" x 11.5" sheet of paper you should still include it. You might want to include a summary sheet in your portfolio and indicate that the full project is available for review. Your choices should summarize as many skills as possible and as much professional growth as possible. In these cases it may be appropriate to include prior good reviews as evidence of your wonderful performance, which is of course deserving of the reward of a pay increase and/or the "corner office."

The key to your success is to let the person reviewing you know why you have a portfolio:

Reason #1—This is how you keep track of your own professional development.

Reason #2—This is designed to save time and assist your reviewer in the process.

Reason #3—it is a tool to help you in the review process.

Be prepared to teach your reviewer how to use your portfolio. Your employer may want to compare you to others in the organization. All these elements and issues can serve you well as you grow and progress as a professional in your field. Don't ever apologize for work you are proud of having done. A portfolio is a great way to break out the different aspects of your career. If you do have an area which needs development then at least your achievements will get some attention as well. Remember the portfolio is a reflection of you—make the most of it.

OOPS, . . . I Blew Them Away

You may be saying—great. They let you talk about your skills and interests based upon your portfolio. They didn't ask you many questions or they spent all their time on one section. They just looked at your portfolio. Is that good or bad?

Remember to use your portfolio to describe your skills, efforts and achievements. Be humble and clear with the interviewer. If the interviewer was overwhelmed with who you are . . . then perhaps you are not well suited for that organization.

It is possible that by using your portfolio, you found out sooner, rather than later that you are over-qualified for the position. Remember that not everybody is using a portfolio, and those who are may not be using them well. You have stood out among your peers. Some companies will practically make you an offer on the spot, others will see you as a threat. Either way, let the truth prevail. Be yourself, don't try to be someone you are not. Your style, knowledge, skills, and interests will be suited for the right company, and your portfolio is a tool designed to help you find the right match for employment in your industry.

5 A MATTER OF STYLE

You are a professional, you have the credentials and the confidence to get ahead. You need to make sure your portfolio projects the same impression. If your portfolio looks sloppy and disorganized, don't even bother to take it to the interview or meeting. Your portfolio must look as clean, organized and professional as you do.

The focus of this section is on style; the look, feel, and presentation of the materials in the portfolio. This section provides some basic guidelines for producing your work samples and other documents in your portfolio by taking a look at:

◆ Working with words and pictures (text and graphics).

◆ Production tips for video and photography.

◆ Physical production of materials using copiers, scanners, and printers.

Text

Have you ever been reading something, and suddenly you realize that you have no idea what you just read for the last four pages? This happens to all of us, but why? Are we not concentrating hard enough, or is the material boring? Your goal in creating your career portfolio is to keep the person reading it awake and interested. You need to make sure that the information is easy to understand , well organized and presented in an interesting style. You want the reader to grasp the meaning of your work without needing to read every word.

Some people write the way they talk—you can almost hear their voices. Your writing needs to have a "voice" when people read it, otherwise everything becomes just words on paper. Be yourself. Your goal is to say what you need to in your professional voice, in a clear, clean, and concise way.

Just as important as the words you use is the look and feel of the text. The following section will give you ideas for improving the style of your words.

- **Organize first**—Decide what you want to say before you begin writing.

- **Create an outline**—Outline the main ideas of what you want to say, then go into detail in each idea.

- **Use "mind-mapping"**—Mind mapping is the process of writing ideas on paper, grouping words and ideas and clustering ideas in a non-linear format.

- **Compose at the computer**—In the 1990s, many people compose and write at the computer, since they can keyboard information faster than they can write it down on paper.

- **Have a friend take notes**—Talk to someone else and have them jot down notes. This is a great way to start getting organized.

- **Use a conversational tone**—Use relaxed and informal style of writing. Write in first person, using I, as in I have done this.... I participated in..., I am managing...

- **Use active vocabulary versus passive**—Active vocabulary projects the idea that you are currently working on something. Compare the use of passive words such as *does, get, show,* to active words like *doing, getting, showing.*

- **Avoid slang and too much jargon**—While it may look impressive, colloquialisms may turn what you are saying into code. Remember, the goal is to make everything clear and easy to understand.

- **Tell the truth**—It's always easier to write what you believe and what you have done, versus making things up and trying to be impressive.

- **Proof your work**—Proofing your work assures a professional look and feel to the documents you produce. Spelling, punctuation or grammar errors can be embarrassing.

◆ **Use bullet points**—Bullets are an easy way to organize information in a readable, concise way. You've probably noticed after reading through this book, that we, the authors, love to use bullet points. Here's a bulleted list, listing some of the reasons to use bullet points:

   ◆ Bullets let you highlight key points in the text.
   ◆ Bullets make it easier for a reader to quickly scan through information.
   ◆ Bullets are often used when you are listing several points or examples.
   ◆ Using bullets can eliminate unnecessary text from sentences.

Now, take a look at the same information, written in paragraph form rather than using bullets, and decide which is easier to read:

> Bullets pull out key information and make it easier for a reader to quickly scan through a lot of information. Bullets are often used when you are listing several points or examples. They also can eliminate unnecessary text from sentences.

Elements of Text

◆ Fonts.
◆ Margins, tabs and spacing.
◆ White space.

Text areas of the portfolio:

◆ Management Philosophy.
◆ Goals.
◆ Résumé.
◆ Work samples.
◆ Community Service.
◆ References.

- Professional memberships and services.
- Exhibit cards.
- Labels for photos and video.

Fonts

The look and style of the letters in your documents come from the fonts. Fonts are one of the simplest ways to control the look of your document, and can be used to let your creativity and personality flow onto the page.

Serif vs. Sans Serif Fonts—There are thousands of fonts available these days. All of these fonts fall into two major categories: Serif or Sans Serif. Each of these groups has a different look and can be used to emphasize specific pieces of information in the document.

Serif fonts have the little flourishes at the ends of letters. The font you are reading now is a serif font called Minion. Notice the curve of an "a" or the edges on a "T".

Examples of serif fonts are:

Times New Roman   Bookman Old Style   Courier New

Sans serif fonts don't have the flourishes and curves in the letters.

Examples of sans serif fonts are:

Arial   Humanist   **Dom Casual**   **Enterprise**

There are no strict rules for the use of fonts, but here are some general guidelines:

- **Use serif fonts for body text**—Serif fonts are easier to read because our eyes use the little flourishes on letters to distinguish the letters. Most of the books you read are in a serif typestyle.

- **Use sans serif fonts for headings**—Sans serif fonts are often used for headings and titles rather than text. They are used to capture interest and draw attention to a particular section.

- ◆ **USE ALL CAPS SPARINGLY**— USING ALL CAPITALS CAN BE DISTRACTING AND HARD TO READ.

- ◆ **Don't be afraid to experiment with different fonts**— Find one that says something about your personality, be it *elegant*, **bold**, stylish, **or slightly wild.** Just remember, it must be readable. You don't want your reader struggling to see what the text says. If text is hard to read, we usually stop reading and skip to something else, which could cause someone to bypass some very important information about you. Consider using this type of font in the title or heading section.

- ◆ **Don't** mix too *many* fonts together *in* a document—Try to stick to one font for text and another for headings. Your work can look jumbled if you use too many variations.

- ◆ **Bold and Italic**—The same goes for **bold** and *italic:* Use them sparingly, when you need something emphasized.

- ◆ **Avoid underlining text!**—<u>Underlining is a tool that was used in the era of the typewriter, when we didn't have bold and italic.</u> Don't use it.

- ◆ **Use a proportional font**—Speaking of typewriters, have you ever noticed how every letter on a typewritten document takes up the same amount of space? Proportional fonts will take up less space, let you fit more on a page, and are easier to read. In the sample below, both paragraphs are set in 12 pitch size, but the non-proportional looks bigger:

```
This text is an example of a non-pro-
portional font. Every character or
space takes up the same amount of
space.(Courier)
```

This text is an example of a proportional font. Each character takes up as much room as it needs. (Minion)

- ◆ **Leave only one period after a space**— Remember the typing rule about leaving two spaces after a period? Two spaces were used so you could easily see the end of a sentence in the typewriter age. With the advent of word processors and proportional fonts, we don't need the extra space. You may think it's a hard habit to break, but it is actually very easy to do.

◆ **Choose the correct font sizes**—The size of the font also affects the readability of the document. The most common size is 12 pitch. This book is written in 12 pitch font to make it easy to read at a glance. 10 pitch is the smallest size we recommend using on résumés and other documents. Any smaller, and it is very hard to read. The text in footers and headers can be smaller than 10 pitch, as long as they are still readable.

◆ **Watch the size of headings**—Most headings are printed in 16 to 18 pitch. Make sure your heading isn't too big for the text; meaning, don't combine 18 pitch headings with 10 pitch text.

◆ **Use spell checking**— All good word processors contain a program to check spelling. Use this to correct typing and spelling mistakes. OK, this is an obvious step, but it's amazing how many documents we see where this simple, convenient step was overlooked. Typos look bad, (especially on the front page of your portfolio!)

◆ **Don't rely on the spell checker**—Too many people rely on the spell checker to catch all their mistakes. Unfortunately the spell checker can't recognize words that are spelled correctly but misused in a sentence.

(You no that I'm talking about don't ewe?— You **know** what I'm talking about don't **you?**)

◆ **Single space your text**—You're probably familiar with single and double spacing. Double spacing is commonly used for reports, but single spacing should be used for most of the documents in your portfolio. Generally, you leave a double space between headings and the body of the text.

◆ **Use customized line spacing**—If you "get into" designing the look of your documents, you may discover that a double space after a heading is too much space. If you really want to customize your document, play with settings for the *space above* or *below* the text. This command is often found in the same location as the single or double spacing commands, and can be used to add extra spacing before or after a heading.

Which of the following combinations looks best to you?

Work Philosophy: *(single spaced)*
I believe that every person should receive excellent customer service.

Work Philosophy: *(double spaced)*

I believe that every person should receive excellent customer service.

Work Philosophy: *(6 points)*
I believe that every person should receive excellent customer service.

Margins, Tabs, and Spacing

The margins, tabs, and spacing you use in a document will change depending on what you are producing. Keep in mind how the document will be used when setting up the page.

Here are some general rules:

◆ **Use a generous margin around the page**—Allow a generous margin around your page, generally 3/4" to 1" around the entire page. Don't make your margins any smaller than 1/2", or your page will look crowded. Many people like to make notes in the margins of a résumé during an interview, and good use of white space in the form of margins allows this. Wider margins also give documents a clean and open look.

◆ **Don't be afraid to go to a second page**—Two or three balanced, open pages look much better than one cramped page. Keep in mind, the information in your documents should be important. Don't go to two pages when you can trim out unnecessary details.

- ◆ **Get to know your word processor**—Look for the easy ways to center and indent information.
- ◆ **Keep the style consistent**—Decide on a look and style for your portfolio documents, and then stick with it. Use the same margins, fonts and spacing on these documents.

Headers and Footers

Headers and **footers** are areas of text that appear at the top and bottom of a page, outside the normal space used to enter information. Headers and footers are used to print text that should appear on each page of a document, such as page numbers, dates, titles, or names. In this book, the page numbers and the chapter title appear in the footer. If you are planning to duplex a document (print on both sides of a page,) you should use the **mirror margin** settings to have information in your headers and/or footers appear on the opposite sides of a left- and right-facing page.

Header and footer information is entered separately from regular text, and usually has tab settings preset to print information left-justified, centered, or right-justified on the page.

Text placed in a header or footer should be in a smaller font, usually 7 to 9 dpi. You may want to print a line between the header or footer and the main body of text to keep them separated.

Here's an example of a page with footers:

Heading

a;sdlkfjaslfasd;lfkasjd;a;
a;akdjflakd;falksdlsklds
a;lskfjakjadlksjdaiejle;liej
a;lsdifasifaslfeifalea;sfehi
a;ldkfafeias;fiefnefiefnlis
a;lfiealisejlaieja fie efeifflie
;lkjlkjlsdfjaieja;lifjaelieff;
aife iefeif ejfiaef;alsife iefj
;alkjlakaieaslifefisefie asie
a;lkfjaslf slfkjsfljs ssl sf; slf
;lkjaliefj idfjle;slfekajsd;flkja

Michael Heroux　　*Feasibility Study*
Pg. 10　　　　　　　*4/26/96*

◆ **Include your name and the page number on each page**—If your document is two or more pages long, include your name and a page number in the header or footer of each page.

White Space

You'll hear graphic designers and desktop publishers constantly babbling about the correct use of white space. No, white space isn't the inside of a padded cell or blizzard conditions in the Midwest; rather, white space is the unprintable areas that appear in and around the text and graphics on a page.

When you make the margins wider in a document, you are increasing the amount of white space on the page. Take a look at some of the computer manuals and documentation you've got lying around, and you'll see lots of variations on the use of white space. Here are some examples:

<table>
<tr><td>

Heading

alskfja;sdlfkajsdlkjkjlkjllkjlkjlkjlkjfkajf
a;lskja;lfjdifdsjhgf;lkjlkjk lkhghgfas;dlf
;asf;lkajflkjfslkfalkfjslkfjsfkjas;lfklfas
f;alkfjalfjlsjwifjweifjwoieifjselfijsalfi
lfjadflksjflkdjflskdjlsdkfjsldkjasld
a;lsdkfjaei afieffg;lkjkj ;lkjhgfghl;aeijij

Subheading

a;ieijeiwoeiruoLjijijifle;eijeil;gfhjgfge
eiuoijl;ij;li iijilhgkwwjhgfjhokerjisefe
aa;dlfkaasloiuoiuoiukjhgfjhgdas;dja;s
;al;lk;lk;lk;lkdkfaj;dlfjhgfjhgfkaj asdkfj
a;lkfaipoipoppjd;kjhgfhjklkadfjalkdfa
aa;lkajsdlksjlskjlskfslkfkaslkasdjflkdasa

</td><td>

Heading

a;lkj lkldskjfaldkkj ;lkj;lkfjasla;
akdjfdls;j jkj a;lkj;lkjlkekfjklef
sdflasjflskdfslfjwiefjlseifjeslifja
dflkjasdlfjwoioifjaslfijaselfejal
sd;lfjasdfliajfleijsldijsdalifjsefi
a;slkdfjas;lkj;lkj;lkj;;kjkjk dfkasa

Subheading

lkdgjie;lkj ;lkjl;dlkj kjkfjeiqoe
eieji;lkj;lkjrkj lkjegiejaseifjieji
a;lsdkfk;lj;lkj;ljhkjhkjald ksdf
a;dkjhkjh;lkj;lkj;kflkajsflakjf;a
;fafaklijijlijlilikjlief;efiasjliejfe
dslkfjaslfkjaflaseijasf sdfasdkfjas

</td></tr>
</table>

Figure #1   Figure #2

Figure #1 contains very little white space and looks cramped. Compare it to Figure #2 where we added a wide left margin.

<table>
<tr><td>

Heading

alskfja;sdlfkajsdlkjkjlkjllkjlkjlk
a;lskja;lfjdifdsjhgf;lkjlkjk lkhg
;asf;lkajflkjfslkfalkfjslkfjsfk;lfs
f;alkfjalfjlsjwifjweifjwoiselfijsaa;

Subheading
a;ieijeiwoeoLjijijifle;eijeil;gfl
a;lkajldfkaldfslfifeliajowiwak
ja;lsdkjfasljaiejlsifasjlfsadfk
;lkjahkjshoqoiweqwuroqiwpi
qopeurorpquworiweoioqieqp
poeriulkdvksdviahoeifjaeflae
aslfaweoadvllldfahifewofjskdlf;
asfawookokoiuafjkawiouowkdjl

</td></tr>
</table>

Figure #3

Figure #3 adds side headings to the text to make the headings stand out.

Heading	**Heading**
alskfja;sdlfkajsdlkjkjlkjllkjlkjlkjl a;lskja;lfjdifdsjhgf;lkjlkjk gfas;dl ;asf;lkajflkjfslkfalslkfjsfkjas;lfklfa f;alkfjalfjlsjwifjwjwoieifjselfijsalfi lfjadflksjflkdjflsjlsdkfjsldkjasld a;lsdkfjaei afieffkj ;lkjhgfghl;aeij	a;lkj lkldskjfaldkkj ;lkj;lkfjas akdjfdls;j jkj a;lkj;lkjlkejklef sdflasjflskdfslfjwilseifjeslifja dflkjasdlfjwoioiflfijaselfejal sd;lfjasdflik kkfjsl ljsdifjsefi a;slkdfjas;lkj;lkj;lkj;;kjkjk dsa
Subheading	**Subheading**
a;ieijeiwoeiruoifle;eijeil;gfhjgfge	lkdgjie;lkj ;lkjl;dlkj kjkfje eieji;lkj;lkjrkj lkjegie kjkjeji a;lsdkfk;lj;lkj;ljhkjhkjalddf a;dkjhkjh;lkj;lkj;kflkajkjf;a ;fafaklijiljiljlilikjliefj;esjliejfe dslkfjaslfkjaflaseijasf sdsdkfjas

Figure #4	**Figure #5**

Placement of graphics is another important consideration in the use of white space.Keep pictures aligned with text if possible as in Figure 4. You can also add interest to a page by adding accent lines as in Figure 5.

Visual Media —Working With Pictures and Video

A picture is worth a thousand words. . . If so, it's really important to get your pictures to look their best in order to convey the right impression. There's no question that we learn more quickly from pictures than from words on a page. Like anything else in your portfolio, pictures and video should demonstrate your ability to perform a specific skill or competency, and should be used when words won't convey this or would take too long.

Photographs

Photographs are used to emphasize your work. Take the best shots that demonstrate your work, and don't include too many photos. Photographs can be useful when you want to:

- **Display a finished product** —elegantly decorated cakes, displays or booths created.
- **Put your talents on display**—public speaking, training sessions, anywhere you are in action.

Tips for Taking Better Photographs:

- **You should appear in the photo when possible**—This provides proof that it's your work, not someone else's.
- **Pay attention to film speed**—100 speed film is good for outdoor shots where you don't need a flash. When shooting indoors, use 200 or 400 speed film, and use a flash.
- **Get close**—Get close to your subject (unless you're photographing wild animals!) Use telephoto shots to get closer if needed.
- **Fill the field**—Use the field finder on the camera and completely fill the picture with the product. Again, get close to the subject!
- **Watch where you stand**—Don't shoot pictures into light. The light meter of a camera adjusts for the brightest light, often making the real subject of the picture too dark.
- **Watch your background**—Most people look a little strange with a flower arrangement for a hat or a pole growing out of their head!
- **Be prepared**—Try out the equipment before you have to take the picture (i.e. know how the equipment works before a critical moment, so you don't forget to take off the lens cap, or find out you have dead batteries in your flash!)
- **Use a tripod**—Tripods keep your work steady and prevent blurry pictures.
- **Consider getting a special camera holder**—If you will be taking lots of still shots of products sitting on a table, make a $35 investment in a camera holder, specifically designed for taking overhead pictures.

Using Video

Video can be used when you want to show examples of yourself in action. Video takes pictures and adds sound. Keep in mind that no one *really* enjoys watching home videos, so keep your video short, to the point, and make it worth watching. Limit your video to 3, 5, 10, or 20 minutes segments. No one is going to sit through more than a 20-minute video.

Tips for Better Videos:

◆ **Tips for photos also apply to video.**

◆ **Emphasize your skills**—Keep the emphasis of your video on your skills, not on your production abilities.

◆ **Be prepared**—Always test out equipment ahead of time, especially if you are borrowing the equipment. It's always good to have extra batteries and an extension cord handy.

◆ **Watch your lighting**—Make sure the lighting is correct.

◆ **Label the video**—Indicate the subject and the length of video clips.

Tips for Looking Your Best in Front of a Lens:

Your looks:

◆ Get a good night's rest!! Weariness and stress are visible. Makeup can only cover so much.

◆ Make sure your hair looks neat and attractive—If you need it cut, do it several days in advance.

◆ Gentlemen—be careful shaving, avoid scrapes and cuts. Watch out for "five o'clock" shadow.

◆ Women—wear make up as usual. If you wear heavy liner on your lower eye lid—go lightly or avoid it so that you do not look like a raccoon.

Clothing choices:

◆ Wear a proper fitting suit and shirt.

- Turtle necks often make people look—like turtles in two dimensions.

- Darker tones make the body look thinner.

- Avoid Navy blue. It shows everything and appears murky.

- Avoid wearing black and white in color photos.

- Avoid wearing white shirts if possible—it can produce a glare.

- Wear a suit jacket for a serious look.

- Make sure your clothes are not too tight. If you have recently gained weight, a new larger shirt will mask the gain better than a tight-fitting outfit.

- Ties should not be remarkably distinctive unless it is a signature look.

- Keep your jewelry to a minimum.

Production Tools—Copiers, Scanners, and Printers

Copiers, scanners and printers are the most common tools you'll use to produce your portfolio. Here are some tips for making their output look as good as possible:

Copiers

- **Clean the machine**—Take a bottle of glass cleaner and a cloth with you the next time you go to make copies. Clean the glass on the machine and you'll find that your final copies will be much clearer.

- **Align the paper**—Center the page on the copier, and make sure the paper is straight on the copier. Nothing is more annoying than crooked copies!

- **Enlarge small fonts**—If the original document is in 10 pitch or smaller type, you must enlarge it to make it easier to read.

- **Copying small pieces of paper**—If you're copying something smaller than 8 1/2" by 11", be sure to put a white piece of paper behind the document so the background is clear. If necessary, tape the original to the paper to hold it centered. If you are trimming the copy from a larger size, be sure to use scissors. Think neat.

- **Color copying**—Color copying is expensive. Look at the project and determine if you really need color in your work sample. Use color copying when you want to accent something special.

- **Consider scanning as an alternative**—It's hard to copy photographs, except black and white. You should scan color pictures for higher quality.

- **When in doubt, ask for professional help**—The staff at copy centers are usually happy to assist you with your copying.

Scanning Equipment

- **Scanning is often a good alternative to photocopying**—it can produce a clearer picture. Combined with a color printer, it can also be a cheaper alternative to color copying.

- **Resolution**—Scanning is measured in dpi—dots per inch. The higher the dpi, the more detailed and sharper the picture. Use no less than 300 dpi, preferably 600 dpi or higher when scanning.

- **Flatbed scanners vs. hand scanners**—Flatbed scanners allow you to copy larger areas of information at a time, and provide better quality than hand scanners. They provide higher resolution and less hassle.

- **Scan certificates and degrees**—For a better look, consider scanning certificates and degrees; they copy official seals better than a copier.

Paper and Printing

Paper

As you choose the paper you'll use in your portfolio, keep in mind that the main purpose of the paper is to enhance the text and graphics in the document, making it easier to read. It can also be used to distinguish you from other people and can capture a bit of your style. Here are some guidelines for selecting paper:

♦ **Use high quality, 20 lb. paper**—Higher weight paper has a better feel and look. It also helps keep printing from showing through to the other side.

♦ **Don't use fax paper or any type of thermal paper**— Thermal paper will fade and age. Make copies of any faxes.

♦ **Paper color** —Use subtle colors, nothing harsh. Use the same paper consistently throughout the portfolio. Use color to draw attention to items you want to emphasize. Don't overuse colored paper; limit yourself to a maximum of three different colors. White should be your primary color.

Printing

♦ **Use a high quality printer**—Good printers can produce 300 to 600 dpi (dots per inch) resolution. The higher the dpi, the higher the quality of the document.

♦ **Working with inkjet printers**—If you are printing on an ink jet printer, use paper that's been designed for ink jets, or paper that says it's compatible. Ink jet paper is designed to absorb the ink and give you a clearer, sharper image than regular laser jet paper.

♦ **Color printing**—Use color printing sparingly to accent important information.

♦ **Don't use dot-matrix printers.**

Tabs and Labels

Here are some ideas to keep in mind when creating the tabs and labels used in the portfolio:

◆ **Buy standard size labels**—Avery brand labels are the most popular brand of labels. Most word processors can automatically set up a document based on common sizes of Avery brand labels. If you buy another brand of labels, be sure they have the same label measurements as the Avery brand. Most word processing packages have pre-set templates which layout the page's margins and space. Setting up labels can be as simple as entering a number off the box.

◆ **Buy labels designed for printers**—When buying labels, be sure to buy printer labels rather than copier labels. Each may contain the same number of labels, but the layout is different. Laser printers have a margin around the edges of the paper that are unprintable, and laser labels accommodate this margin. Copier labels usually go right to the edge of the paper, which can cause alignment nightmares.

◆ **Use clear labels**—Consider using clear labels instead of white for a more professional look.

◆ **Don't waste labels**—Labels cost money, so don't waste them. Print your labels to a blank sheet of paper first, then hold them up to the light against a page of labels to check the alignment. Make any necessary adjustments and repeat the process until the labels are aligned, then use the real thing.

Send Us Your Success Story

Our research continues. We are interested in your stories about using the portfolio. We want to hear your experiences and opinions. Tell us how your friends and family reacted. Let us know what you did to improve the portfolio's layout or contents. Share with us how you used the portfolio with your employer and how your organization reacted.

We are interested in the types of work samples you used and how you produced quality copies.Tell us what you would like to see developed or improved in the portfolio. Our next book will expand on the electronic portfolio. If you have any questions, ideas or comments we would love to hear them. Let us know how we can help.

Please send your success story to:

Learnovation

My Portfolio
11438 Cherry Blossom West Drive
Fishers, In 46038-2417

or **E-mail** us at: **103327.2455@compuserve.com**

Visit our web page to learn more about career mechanics and other's portfolio experiences.

http://www.learnovation.com

Index